ASQ-3™ Learning Activities

by

Elizabeth Twombly, M.S.

and

Ginger Fink, M.A.

Baltimore • London • Sydney

Paul H. Brookes Publishing Co.
Post Office Box 10624
Baltimore, Maryland 21285-0624

www.brookespublishing.com

Visit www.agesandstages.com to learn more about the complete ASQ system.

Typeset by Auburn Associates, Inc., Baltimore, Maryland.
Manufactured in the United States of America by
Versa Press, Inc., East Peoria, Illinois.

Cover image, as well as images in this book and on the accompanying CD-ROM, © istockphoto.com and © Veer.

See the photocopying release on page xi for specific conditions in which photocopying is permitted.

For other questions pertaining to the ASQ, please visit www.agesandstages.com or contact the Subsidiary Rights Department, Paul H. Brookes Publishing Co., Post Office Box 10624, Baltimore, MD 21285-0624, USA; 1-410-337-9580; rights@brookespublishing.com.

Library of Congress Cataloging-in-Publication Data
Twombly, Elizabeth.
    ASQ-3 (TM) learning activities / by Elizabeth Twombly and Ginger Fink.
        p.   cm.
    ISBN 978-1-59857-246-9 (pbk.)—ISBN 1-59857-246-6 (pbk.)
    1. Child development—Testing.   2. Infants—Development—Testing.   3. Child development deviations—Diagnosis.   4. Early childhood education—
Activity programs.   I. Fink, Ginger.   II. Title.
    RJ51.D48T86 2013
    618.92'85882—dc23
                                                                                                                                2012012195

British Library Cataloguing in Publication data are available from the British Library.

2022   2021   2020   2019   2018

10   9   8   7   6

Contents

Contents

Contents of the Accompanying CD-ROM

About This CD-ROM
About *ASQ-3 Learning Activities*
Hello, Parent!

0–2 months
Communication
Gross Motor
Fine Motor
Problem Solving
Personal-Social

2–4 months
Communication
Gross Motor
Fine Motor
Problem Solving
Personal-Social

4–8 months
Communication
Gross Motor
Fine Motor
Problem Solving
Personal-Social

8–12 months
Communication
Gross Motor
Fine Motor
Problem Solving
Personal-Social

12–16 months
Communication
Gross Motor
Fine Motor
Problem Solving
Personal-Social

16–20 months
Communication
Gross Motor
Fine Motor
Problem Solving
Personal-Social

20–24 months
Communication
Gross Motor
Fine Motor
Problem Solving
Personal-Social

24–30 months
Communication
Gross Motor
Fine Motor
Problem Solving
Personal-Social

30–36 months
Communication
Gross Motor
Fine Motor
Problem Solving
Personal-Social

36–42 months
Communication
Gross Motor
Fine Motor
Problem Solving
Personal-Social

42–48 months
Communication
Gross Motor
Fine Motor
Problem Solving
Personal-Social

48–54 months
Communication
Gross Motor
Fine Motor
Problem Solving
Personal-Social

54–60 months
Communication
Gross Motor
Fine Motor
Problem Solving
Personal-Social

About the Authors
ASQ Training
ASQ Ordering Guide
End User License Agreement

Acknowledgments

We wish to acknowledge the continued encouragement that Jane Squires gave us to complete this project. In addition, we wish to acknowledge and thank our many professional friends in Hawaii for their contributions to this project and their continued support.

About the Authors

Elizabeth Twombly, M.S., lives in Eugene, Oregon, and is a faculty member of the Early Intervention Program at the University of Oregon, Eugene. Prior to working in the field of early intervention, Ms. Twombly spent many years working with young children in environmental education, child care, and preschool programs on the East and West coasts. She is a contributing author on *Ages & Stages Questionnaires®, Third Edition (ASQ-3™): A Parent-Completed Child Monitoring System* (Squires & Bricker, Paul H. Brookes Publishing Co., 2009) and coauthor on *Ages & Stages Questionnaires®: Social-Emotional, Second Edition (ASQ:SE-2): A Parent-Completed Child Monitoring System for Social-Emotional Behaviors* (with Squires & Bricker, Paul H. Brookes Publishing Co., 2015). For more than 20 years, Ms. Twombly has served on the ASQ research team, and she trains across the nation and internationally on the implementation of developmental and social-emotional screening tools in home visiting programs and health and educational settings.

Ginger Fink, M.A., has worked in the field of early childhood education for more than 30 years. She has worked in many capacities as a teacher, director, curriculum developer, and teacher educator. Ms. Fink is a private consultant in the area of parent–child programs and teacher education strategies. She worked for the Kamehameha Schools, Honolulu, Hawaii, as the curriculum developer for a statewide network of community-based parent–child learning programs. She also worked extensively with Head Start programs as a teacher and program director intermittently between 1966 and 1975 and as a disabilities specialist between 1997 and 2000 for the Region X Training and Technical Assistance network. Ms. Fink also served as the training coordinator for the ASQ developmental screening system for the University of Oregon, Eugene. In addition to private consultation, she teaches early childhood courses at Clackamas Community College, Oregon City, Oregon.

Photocopying Release

Purchasers of *ASQ-3™ Learning Activities* are granted permission to photocopy the learning activities sheets and "Hello, Parent!" letter solely in the course of their agency's or practice's service provision to families. Photocopies may only be made from an original *ASQ-3™ Learning Activities* book or CD-ROM.

Each branch office or physical site that will be using *ASQ-3 Learning Activities* must purchase its own original book with CD-ROM; neither the book nor the CD-ROM may be shared among sites.

Electronic reproduction and distribution of the sheets and letter is prohibited except as otherwise explicitly authorized (see Frequently Asked Questions in the book [pp. xiii–xv] as well as the End User License Agreement included with the CD-ROM).

The *ASQ-3 Learning Activities* materials are meant to be used to facilitate a screening or monitoring program and to support child development. These materials may not be used in a way contrary to the family-oriented philosophies of the ASQ developers. None of the ASQ materials may be reproduced to generate revenue for any program or individual.

Unauthorized use beyond this privilege is prosecutable under federal law. You will see the copyright protection line at the bottom of each photocopiable page.

For more information about ASQ or to contact the Subsidiary Rights Department, go to www.agesand stages.com.

Frequently Asked Questions

These are some of the frequently asked questions that users pose to Brookes Publishing. The information that follows is primarily focused on rights and permissions associated with using *ASQ-3™ Learning Activities*.

PHOTOCOPYING

Can *ASQ-3 Learning Activities* sheets be photocopied?

Yes, the *ASQ-3 Learning Activities* sheets (including the "Hello, Parent!" letter) may be photocopied for use at a single physical site with all of the children and families served by that site. They may not be photocopied to share among different sites. See the Photocopying Release (p. xi) for certain restrictions.

ASQ-3 LEARNING ACTIVITIES BOOKS NEEDED

My organization has many locations throughout the state. How many ASQ-3 Learning Activities books do I need to buy?

Each branch office or physical site that will be using *ASQ-3 Learning Activities* must purchase its own book with accompanying CD-ROM; the book and CD-ROM cannot be shared among sites.

I understand that use of *ASQ-3 Learning Activities* is site specific. How is a *site* defined?

A site is a single physical location, such as an office. An organization may have various sites, such as the downtown office, the east branch, and the north branch. The sites may be located in the same city or town, the same country, the same state, or even different states. For instance, the University of Michigan has three campuses in Michigan: Ann Arbor, Flint, and Dearborn. Each campus is a different site; the main campus in Ann Arbor cannot purchase *ASQ-3 Learning Activities* and then share copies of the book or CD-ROM or their contents with the two branch campuses in other cities. Even on one campus, there are different sites. For example, if the School of Social Work wanted to use *ASQ-3 Learning Activities* and the School of Education also wanted to use *ASQ-3 Learning Activities*, they each must purchase their own *ASQ-3 Learning Activities* book with CD-ROM because they are separate departments located in different buildings.

Head Start programs are another example. Even though there are dozens of Head Start programs across the United States and they are all part of the same organization, the main office cannot purchase one copy of the *ASQ-3 Learning Activities* book with CD-ROM to share with all of the sites. Each site must own an original *ASQ-3 Learning Activities* book with CD-ROM. Some ASQ-3 users are pediatricians with more than one office in the same town; each office must own an original *ASQ-3 Learning Activities* book with CD-ROM rather than sharing materials between the multiple offices in the same town.

Frequently Asked Questions

POSTING

Can I post the *ASQ-3 Learning Activities* sheets from the CD-ROM on my program's computer network?

The learning activities sheets, "Hello, Parent!" letter, and ordering guide can be posted on your program's local area network (LAN) or intranet if **only** people in your organization at a single physical site have access to the LAN or intranet. Employees can then print and use the sheets, letter, and ordering guide as needed from their own computers at that single physical site but can only access these items from that single physical site. Remote access from another physical site, including by virtual private network (VPN), file transfer protocol (FTP), tunneling protocols, or other means, is not permitted.

Can I post *ASQ-3 Learning Activities* on my web site or my organization's web site?

No. Posting the *ASQ-3 Learning Activities* sheets, "Hello, Parent!" letter, and ordering guide on any web site (password protected or otherwise) is not permitted.

E-MAILING

Can I e-mail the *ASQ-3 Learning Activities* sheets to a family or my colleague?

The *ASQ-3 Learning Activities* sheets may be e-mailed to a family in the course of your service provision to them. However, e-mailing the sheets to a professional or colleague is **not** permitted.

Can I e-mail the "Hello, Parent!" letter to a family?

Yes, you may e-mail the letter to a family in the course of your service provision to them. However, e-mailing the letter to a professional or colleague is **not** permitted.

EXTRACTING

Can I use some of *ASQ-3 Learning Activities* in a document or materials that I am creating?

Brookes Publishing appreciates interest in *ASQ-3 Learning Activities*. However, you need written permission from Brookes Publishing before adapting, translating, reformatting, reprinting, or reproducing (except as covered by the *ASQ-3 Learning Activities* Photocopying Release) the learning activities sheets, any related materials, or any part thereof in any way. To apply for permission, please complete the Permission Request Form online at http://www.brookespublishing.com.

CD-ROM

What can I do with the *ASQ-3 Learning Activities* CD-ROM?

The CD-ROM can be treated like a more durable version of the *ASQ-3 Learning Activities* book. This means you may print and photocopy the learning activities sheets or related materials as needed under the terms specified in the Photocopying Release and the End User License Agreement on the CD-ROM. The learning activities sheets, "Hello, Parent!" letter, and ordering guide can be posted on a LAN or intranet. Only people in your organization at a single physical site can have access to the LAN or intranet and can only access the materials from that single physical site.

Are the learning activities sheets on the CD-ROM interactive?

No, the learning activities sheets on the CD-ROM are not fillable or interactive. The PDF files on the CD-ROM are basically a more durable version of the paper sheets in the book. You can use the CD-ROM to print the sheets and then photocopy them as needed.

KEYCODE

What is the *ASQ-3 Learning Activities* keycode?

The *ASQ-3 Learning Activities* keycode is a unique number assigned to your book. This keycode is used to unlock the *ASQ-3 Learning Activities* sheets within a subscription to an ASQ Online system (ASQ Pro or ASQ Enterprise). The keycode is required in order to access online the specific *ASQ-3 Learning Activities* product that a site has purchased.

Where can I find the keycode?

Your keycode is printed on a sticker in your *ASQ-3 Learning Activities* book. The sticker is located on the inside front cover of the book.

How do I use the keycode?

Once your ASQ Online subscription is activated and you have a login and password, the program administrator may enter the *ASQ-3 Learning Activities* keycode on the program's profile within the system so that you may begin using the learning activities sheets. Please visit http://www.agesandstages.com for additional information.

TRANSLATIONS

I work with a population that does not speak and/or read English. Is *ASQ-3 Learning Activities* available in other languages?

Yes, *ASQ-3 Learning Activities* currently is available in Spanish from Brookes Publishing. Other languages are in development and may become available; for the latest information, please see http://www.agesandstages.com.

I am conducting a research project with a population that does not speak and/or read English and I would like to use *ASQ-3 Learning Activities*. Can I get permission to translate the learning activities sheets myself?

Brookes Publishing is pleased to consider requests to translate some or all of the learning activities sheets. Please contact the Subsidiary Rights Department at rights@brookespublishing.com.

MORE INFORMATION

How do I get more information about *ASQ-3 Learning Activities* usage and rights and permissions?

More information is available at http://www.agesandstages.com. If your question is not answered by the details provided online, please e-mail your inquiry to Brookes Publishing's Subsidiary Rights Department at rights@brookespublishing.com. E-mails are answered as quickly as possible. However, due to the volume of inquiries received, please be advised that it may be approximately 4–6 weeks before you receive a response.

About Your Keycode

The *ASQ-3™ Learning Activities* keycode is a unique number assigned to each book with the accompanying CD-ROM. This keycode is used to unlock the *ASQ-3 Learning Activities* sheets within a subscription to an ASQ Online system (ASQ Pro for single sites; ASQ Enterprise for multisite programs). The keycode is required in order to access online the specific *ASQ-3 Learning Activities* product that a site has purchased.

For instance, a program that has purchased *ASQ-3 Learning Activities* in English has a keycode that will enable it to successfully access the *ASQ-3 Learning Activities* sheets within its ASQ Pro or ASQ Enterprise subscription. The program will **not** be able to use *ASQ-3 Learning Activities* in Spanish within the ASQ Online system if it has not purchased that product. However, if the program decides at any time to purchase *ASQ-3 Learning Activities* in Spanish, the program administrator may enter the keycode provided and begin using the additional learning activities sheets.

Keycodes may not be shared between sites. Each keycode may be used only once. After a keycode has been entered in ASQ Online, it will not unlock learning activities for another account. It is strongly recommended that you keep your keycode secure because it is required to successfully use your subscriptions for online management.

Your keycode is printed on a sticker that is inside the front cover of your *ASQ-3 Learning Activities* book. Once your ASQ Online subscription is activated and you have a login and password, the program administrator may enter the keycode on the program's profile within the system so that the program may begin using the learning activities sheets.

Please visit http://www.agesandstages.com for additional information.

Introduction

Welcome to *ASQ-3™ Learning Activities!* These activities have been designed to coordinate with *Ages & Stages Questionnaires®, Third Edition (ASQ-3™): A Parent-Completed Child Monitoring System* (Squires & Bricker, 2009). These simple activities are designed to provide parents, home visitors, teachers, and others with quick, inexpensive ideas for learning games and interactions that enhance the growth and development of infants and young children. These activities are written in simple language and use materials that most families have on hand at home.

In addition to supporting areas of development, it is our hope that these activities will strengthen the parent–child relationship. To this end, the activities are designed to be playful, fun, and affectionate. We hope that these activities will bring laughter and joy to the family. Although *ASQ-3 Learning Activities* are designed for use with the ASQ system, they are appropriate to use independent of a screening or monitoring program.

AGES & STAGES QUESTIONNAIRES AND THE *ASQ-3 LEARNING ACTIVITIES*

Ages & Stages Questionnaires, Third Edition (ASQ-3), are a series of parent-completed questionnaires that screen and monitor a child's development between 1 month and 5½ years of age. The results of a questionnaire indicate if a child is currently developing at an age-appropriate level or if he or she should receive a more in-depth assessment (e.g., from a local Part C early intervention [EI] or Part B early childhood special education [ECSE] agency) to determine eligibility to receive specialized services. ASQ-3 screens development in the areas of communication, gross motor, fine motor, problem solving, and personal-social skills. Each questionnaire includes a section that elicits input on overall parent concerns that may also result in the need for a referral to a primary health care provider or EI/ECSE service provider.

Because the questionnaires are typically completed by a parent or caregiver rather than a professional, this screening system provides an inexpensive method for screening and monitoring a child's development. Screening with ASQ-3 elicits three potential results for each area of development:

- **Above cutoff:** The child's score is above the cutoff, and the child's development appears to be proceeding typically at this point in time.

- **Monitoring zone:** The child's score is close to the cutoff and is in the monitoring zone (between 1 and 2 standard deviations below the mean). It is not unusual for children to have an area score in the monitoring zone because many factors, such as opportunities to practice skills, children's environments, and cultural contexts, may affect children's performance on ASQ-3. However, a child's development should be monitored in any areas that are in the monitoring zone, and additional support (e.g., activities, opportunities to practice) should be provided. Because each state has different eligibility criteria for early intervention or special education services, it is important to consult with local and/or state EI/ECSE providers to determine if scores that fall in the monitoring zone (especially across two or more areas) may warrant a referral.

- **Below cutoff:** The child's score is at or below the cutoff (set at 2 standard deviations below the mean). The child should be referred to a professional for further assessment and to determine if he or she is eligible for EI/ECSE services.

ASQ-3 Learning Activities are designed to be used to follow up with children who receive scores *above the cutoff* or in the *monitoring zone* on ASQ-3. If a child's scores are below the cutoffs and the child is referred and determined *not* eligible for specialized services, the learning activities also can be used. However, these activities are not intended to be a comprehensive intervention that meets the needs of a child with an identified developmental delay. As mentioned previously, these children should be receiving in-depth individualized instruction from an early intervention or early childhood special education provider. If appropriate, the activities could be used to support an intervention program. Additional activities can be found in the *ASQ-3 User's Guide* (pp. 201–223).

ASQ-3 Learning Activities coordinate with ASQ-3 and are grouped according to the age of the child and the area of development. They are organized by age range into 13 sets of activities. Table 1 provides guidelines as to which age range of the learning activities should be provided after screening with ASQ-3.

Table 1. *Ages & Stages Questionnaires, Third Edition (ASQ-3™)* and *ASQ-3™ Learning Activities* age range guidelines

ASQ-3 Interval	ASQ-3 Learning Activities	Page numbers in this book
1 month	0–2 months	1–9
2 months	2–4 months	11–19
4 months	4–8 months	21–29
6 months	4–8 months	21–29
8 months	8–12 months	31–39
9 months	8–12 months	31–39
10 months	8–12 months	31–39
12 months	12–16 months	41–49
14 months	12–16 months	41–49
16 months	16–20 months	51–59
18 months	16–20 months	51–59
20 months	20–24 months	61–69
22 months	20–24 months	61–69
24 months	24–30 months	71–79
27 months	24–30 months	71–79
30 months	30–36 months	81–89
33 months	30–36 months	81–89
36 months	36–42 months	91–99
42 months	42–48 months	101–109
48 months	48–54 months	111–119
54 months	54–60 months	121–129
60 months	54–60 months	121–129

ASQ-3

ASQ-3 LEARNING ACTIVITIES SHEETS

This *ASQ-3 Learning Activities* book includes a "Hello, Parent!" letter (see page xxv) and more than 400 learning activities organized by age range on 65 photocopiable sheets. The accompanying CD-ROM contains the letter and all of the learning activities sheets as printable color PDFs. In addition, ASQ Online subscribers may use the keycode located on the inside front cover of this book to use the learning activities sheets and letter in their online management system (see About Your Keycode on p. xvii for more information).

The learning activities are written at a fourth- to sixth-grade reading level. Each learning activities sheet includes the following elements:

① Developmental area

② Intended age range for use

③ A brief developmental description

④ A series of five to eight age-appropriate activities

⑤ An area for notes

See Figure 1 for a visual guide to a learning activities sheet. Please note that the pronouns *he* and *she* alternate throughout the series of activities, but the activities are intended to be appropriate for either boys or girls. If there are specific guidelines for what age to start an activity (i.e., a narrower range than the overall range of the set), it is noted in the activity.

The letter and sheets may be photocopied from this book or printed and photocopied from the accompanying CD-ROM to share with caregivers. Please see the Photocopying Release on page xi and the End User License Agreement on the CD-ROM for information about how these materials may and may not be used.

There are five learning activities sheets in each set, one for each developmental area in ASQ-3: Communication, Gross Motor, Fine Motor, Problem Solving, and Personal-Social. Although every activity a child engages in can provide opportunities to practice and enhance multiple skills, these activities focus on one specific area at a time so that parents and other caregivers can concentrate their attention on each specific area.

Using the Learning Activities

Following a screening, program staff members have the option of either providing a full set of learning activities sheets to a caregiver (all five sheets) or selecting specific areas based on screening results. For example, a child at 12 months of age may receive ASQ-3 scores well above the cutoffs in the areas of Communication, Gross Motor, Problem Solving, and Personal-Social but receive a score in the monitoring zone in the Fine Motor area. In this case, staff can provide caregivers with a full set of 12–16 month learning activities sheets or with only the 12–16 month Fine Motor learning activities sheet.

The activities provide opportunities for children to develop a variety of skills in each developmental area and to practice skills that are targeted on the ASQ-3 screening; however, these activities should not be considered all inclusive. Children learn from adults in many ways; these are just a few ideas to get parents started and set the stage for positive adult–child interaction. Some may be new; many others are time tested and familiar. We hope that parents will become comfortable with these activities and add new ideas from their own experiences. Home visitors and other professionals are invited to add to these activities or to modify them to meet a specific child's or family's needs. The notes area may be used to add an activity or modification, to share a reminder, or to capture parent feedback.

Supporting Language and Literacy Development

In each set of learning activities, we have included games or activities that support language and literacy development. We hope that some foundations of literacy will be encouraged in every child's home, such

Gross Motor ①

DEVELOPMENTAL AREA

Activities to Help Your Baby Grow and Learn

② 0–2 months

AGE RANGE

③

INFORMATION ABOUT DEVELOPMENT

Your amazing new baby will grow rapidly during these first weeks. Her limbs are held close to her body and her fists are tightly closed. Although her neck is not yet very strong, she will soon want to lift her head, especially while on her tummy. (Your careful supervision is important anytime baby lies on her tummy.) Within a few weeks, she will be able to hold her head up for a few seconds while you hold her up to your shoulder. Her knees are usually pulled up toward her tummy, but soon she will relax and practice kicking.

④

LEARNING ACTIVITIES

Open Wide! — After bath time when your baby is feeling relaxed and awake, hold baby's fists close to her chest, then gently pull them apart to an open position, then pull them closed again. Make a little song about it: "*Close* the baby. Now *open* up the baby. Now *close* the baby. Now *kiss* the baby!" Baby will have fun playing and watching your happy face.

Baby Tummy Time — While baby is on his tummy, lie beside him with your face by his. Hold his fingers and meet his eyes. Talk a bit and sing. Smile and let him know how wonderful he is. What a happy way to visit! Next time place yourself on baby's other side.

Tickle Toes — While your baby is on her back, help her learn about her feet by playing games with her feet and toes. Put her feet together and kiss the bottoms: "Yum yum, what tasty little feet you have!" Nibble her little toes and blow little buzzing sounds into her toes. Be sure to watch baby's face to make sure she's having fun.

Things are Looking Up! — While baby is on his tummy, watch for signs that his head and neck are getting stronger. When baby begins to lift his head, place an interesting toy or a shiny spoon in front of his gaze, and encourage him to raise his head to get a better look. Talk about how strong he is when he lifts his head.

Hide the Mommy (or Daddy) — While baby is lying on her back, place yourself on one side with your face at about her level. Talk to her and call her name: "Hi, little baby. Where's your mommy?" When baby turns her head to your voice, be sure to smile and show a happy face: "You found me!" Now play the game from the other side.

Beautiful Bath Time — While bathing baby, take a little time to give him some extra massage. Talk to him while you gently rub his "special little neck," "rumply little tummy," or "strong back and beautiful bottom." You might also talk as you pat baby dry after the bath. Your hands on these body parts will teach baby about his body, and he will hear the love in your voice.

Notes: ⑤ AREA FOR NOTES

Don't Forget! Activities should be supervised at all times by an adult. Any material, food, or toy given to a young child should be reviewed for safety. Always stay with baby when he is placed on his tummy or in water.

Figure 1. Sample *ASQ-3™ Learning Activities* sheet with guide.

ASQ-3

as experimenting with rhythm and rhymes; gesturing; speaking and listening; reading books, magazines, newspapers, and signs on the street and in stores; experimenting with writing tools by scribbling, drawing, creating grocery lists, and writing letters and cards to loved ones; and so forth. The love and enjoyment of reading as well as success in later formal school situations can be rooted in these early childhood years.

Adapting Learning Activities

Adaptations may be necessary to respectfully support families whose first language is not English or who come from diverse cultural backgrounds. Although these learning activities sheets are available in English and Spanish, we hope that home visitors or parents will feel free to adapt them to other home languages and to add games from their traditions or experiences. All cultures have special favorite baby games, rhymes, and songs. When babies hear these loving sounds, their knowledge of who they are will be strengthened. In some cases, a learning activity may not be something a family might choose to teach. For example, some families may not wish to engage their children with mirrors. Try substitution if a family has a concern about a particular item in an activity. For example, if a family does not want their child to play with food, you could suggest substituting yarn or string for cooked noodles. Respect for the family's values must guide the interactions and choices.

Sharing the Learning Activities with Families

The "Hello, Parent!" letter on page xxv and on the accompanying CD-ROM may help with introducing the learning activities to families. The fourth- to sixth-grade reading level of the learning activities sheets will meet the needs of many families, but other families may need additional support. Activities may need to be demonstrated, illustrated, or shared verbally with families. For example, a home visitor can introduce a new activity to a family each week, bringing specific toys or helping family members gather materials in their home environment. Of course, it is important to consider safety guidelines for children at each developmental level. Although some of the activities include safety precautions, an adult should supervise all activities that involve young children. Use the activities with flexibility, and encourage families to have fun and learn.

REFERENCES

Individuals with Disabilities Education Improvement Act (IDEA) of 2004, PL 108-446, 20 U.S.C. §§ 1400 et seq.
Squires, J., & Bricker, D. (2009). *Ages & Stages Questionnaires®, Third Edition (ASQ-3™): A Parent-Completed Child Monitoring System*. Baltimore, MD: Paul H. Brookes Publishing Co.

Hello, Parent!

Welcome to parenthood, a journey like no other. Your child is special and truly one of a kind, like your experience as a parent. Keep this in mind as you watch your child's growth from day to day. As your baby or child grows, some changes may come quickly and others more slowly. Parenthood will take you through times of challenge and times of joy. One thing is true—life will never be the same! Best wishes to you.

During these early years, you may have concerns about your child's growth, health, or behavior. Make sure to talk to someone, such as a doctor or teacher, about your concerns. Parents all need help now and then. You know your baby best. Concerns and questions about your baby are never silly.

These activities are designed to give you ideas for fun things to do that support your child's learning and growing. Activities can usually be done with just your face and voice or what you have around the house. Many things can be done during the times you are busy with your child anyway, such as mealtime or bath time.

You may notice that there are not any activities that include "screen time" (e.g., movies, television, computers). Studies have shown that too much screen time is linked to later problems with attention, learning, and difficult behaviors. Your baby's brain is growing so fast between birth and 5½ years of age. Activities with real people and real things will help your child learn to talk and listen, move his or her body, and solve problems. Your child can't learn these things from watching television or playing video games.

Here are some things to keep in mind as you try the activities and interact with your child:

- **Be ready to play!** Activities should be fun for both of you. Make sure your child is happy, rested, and not hungry—and that you are, too!

- **Change it.** If a game or activity doesn't work for you, change it around to fit your style, or use what you have on hand that's appropriate.

- **Try family favorites.** You may remember some games or songs from your own childhood. Your child will love these, too. Even though they may not appear on an activity sheet, passing on your very own songs and rhymes to your baby is special and important.

- **Join in the fun.** Invite other family members or friends to join in some of the games and activities. They will probably enjoy getting to know your child, and your child will get to know more about special family and friends.

Don't forget safety! Children are too young to know what is safe and what is not. Your close attention is important to make sure they stay safe while playing and learning.

- Always watch babies and young children in or around water.

- Pay close attention to games or play time while your baby is on his or her stomach. For the first few months, your baby's neck muscles may not be strong enough to lift his or her head and clear the nose and mouth to breathe. Always put baby to sleep on his or her back.

- Always watch any play with strings, cords, long scarves, or anything that might wrap around your child's head or neck.

- Although balloons are fun for children's play, even a deflated balloon can be a choking danger. After playing with balloons or when a balloon breaks, remove it from children right away.

- If you let your child play with a mobile phone, make sure the batteries are removed. Experts are still unsure how mobile phone use may affect the brain, so it is best to be careful.

- Ask your doctor about food allergies. We have tried to avoid any activity that includes foods that may cause an allergic reaction. However, all babies are different, so be alert.

Enjoy your parenting journey! Take a little time each day just to relax with your child and be playful. Your child grows up only once, so these years—although tiring and challenging—should be filled with joy and pleasure.

ASQ-3™ Learning Activities by Elizabeth Twombly and Ginger Fink.

Communication
Activities to Help Your Baby Grow and Learn

0–2 months

Your newborn is already a communicator. He frets and cries if he needs you, and he may gurgle and coo when he's calm. Even wiggles and squirms are part of his communication. Your baby communicates with his eyes as he looks for yours. He seems to be saying, "You are my most important person." Soon your baby will capture your heart with a real smile!

Humming and Holding	Hold your baby close to the skin of your chest or neck. She loves the feel and smell of that wonderful body. As you walk or rock or simply rest, hum a little tune or lullaby. Baby will hear and feel your soft song.
Squirmy Wiggles	Sometimes your baby will frown, squint his little eyes, and tighten up his little tummy. Ask about that as you hold him to your shoulder and gently stroke his body: "Is air in there? Do you need a little burp?"
Happy Talk	When baby seems to be smiling, have a happy talk about it and smile right back: "Look at that smile!" Soon you'll know when your baby is really smiling at you! It's a magic time for both of you.
"Ooo" to You	While baby is rested, relaxed, and looking at your face, softly say a long "ooooooo" sound. Watch how she reacts. When baby is a few weeks old, she may think your "ooooo" face is very interesting and try to make one, too. Soon baby will try to say "ooooooo" back. What a conversation!
Calling, Calling You!	When you are out of sight and baby starts to cry, tell baby that you hear him and that help is on the way: "I hear you, little one, and I'm coming to you." Your baby will learn that your voice is like a promise and that your face will soon appear. How wonderful!
Talking and Teaching	When your baby is awake and relaxed, take a walk around the room or step outside if the weather is nice. Tell her about the people and things in his world: "This is your window. This is your sofa. This is your sister. Look, this is your flower. These are just for you."

Notes:

Don't Forget! Activities should be supervised at all times by an adult. Any material, food, or toy given to a young child should be reviewed for safety.

ASQ-3™ Learning Activities by Elizabeth Twombly and Ginger Fink.
Copyright © 2013 by Paul H. Brookes Publishing Co. All rights reserved.

Gross Motor
Activities to Help Your Baby Grow and Learn

Your amazing new baby will grow rapidly during these first weeks. Her limbs are held close to her body and her fists are tightly closed. Although her neck is not yet very strong, she will soon want to lift her head, especially while on her tummy. (Your careful supervision is important anytime baby lies on her tummy.) Within a few weeks, she will be able to hold her head up for a few seconds while you hold her up to your shoulder. Her knees are usually pulled up toward her tummy, but soon she will relax and practice kicking.

Open Wide!	After bath time when your baby is feeling relaxed and awake, hold baby's fists close to her chest, then gently pull them apart to an open position, then pull them closed again. Make a little song about it: "*Close* the baby. Now *open* up the baby. Now *close* the baby. Now *kiss* the baby!" Baby will have fun playing and watching your happy face.
Baby Tummy Time	While baby is on his tummy, lie beside him with your face by his. Hold his fingers and meet his eyes. Talk a bit and sing. Smile and let him know how wonderful he is. What a happy way to visit! Next time place yourself on baby's other side.
Tickle Toes	While your baby is on her back, help her learn about her feet by playing games with her feet and toes. Put her feet together and kiss the bottoms: "Yum yum, what tasty little feet you have!" Nibble her little toes and blow little buzzing sounds into her toes. Be sure to watch baby's face to make sure she's having fun.
Things Are Looking Up!	While baby is on his tummy, watch for signs that his head and neck are getting stronger. When baby begins to lift his head, place an interesting toy or a shiny spoon in front of his gaze, and encourage him to raise his head to get a better look. Talk about how strong he is when he lifts his head.
Hide the Mommy (or Daddy)	While baby is lying on her back, place yourself on one side with your face at about her level. Talk to her and call her name: "Hi, little baby. Where's your mommy?" When baby turns her head to your voice, be sure to smile and show a happy face: "You found me!" Now play the game from the other side.
Beautiful Bath Time	While bathing baby, take a little time to give him some extra massage. Talk to him while you gently rub his "special little neck," "rumply little tummy," or "strong back and beautiful bottom." You might also talk as you pat baby dry after the bath. Your hands on these body parts will teach baby about his body, and he will hear the love in your voice.

Notes:

Don't Forget! Activities should be supervised at all times by an adult. Any material, food, or toy given to a young child should be reviewed for safety. Always stay with baby when he is placed on his tummy or in water.

Fine Motor
Activities to Help Your Baby Grow and Learn

Your new baby's hands are usually closed in little fists. If you place your finger in her little hand, you will be surprised at the strength of her grip. If you place a small toy in her hand, that grip will help her hold on to it, although it may be only for a very short time. As she grows, her hands will begin to relax. She will find textures and surfaces interesting, so she may move her fingers against cloth or your face or may grasp your hair, even though she has no knowledge that it is attached to you!

Tiny Tugging	While your baby is relaxed and rested, place your finger in baby's fist. Feel baby's grip on your finger. Now slowly tug baby's hand just a bit. If she holds on, relax and tug once more. Tell baby how strong she is. Switch hands and tug again. Make up a little tugging song to sing as you gently tug and relax.
Happy Holder	Give your baby some experience holding different things with different textures. Place different safe items in baby's grip. Let him hold on to a spoon (cool and hard). Later, let baby hold on to the corner of his washcloth (damp and warm). Let him hold on to a toy or a sock. Just letting him hold different things is a way to teach him about the world.
Family Fingers	Let baby play with the members of her family by holding their fingers. Wash hands before playing this game! When Grandma places her finger in baby's hand, she can greet baby and have a little talk: "Hello, beautiful! I'm your grandma, and you are holding on to my finger!" Next, let brother or sister have a turn. Stop when your baby gets tired or starts to fuss.
Happy Hands	After baby's bath, rub some baby oil or lotion on his hands. Gently massage the wrist, palms, and each tiny finger. Tell baby about what you're doing: "I'm rubbing your beautiful little thumb."
Scarf Pull	Place one corner of a smooth scarf or handkerchief in baby's hand. Now pull it through slowly, open it, and let the colors flutter in front of baby's gaze. What a colorful surprise!

Notes:

 Don't Forget! Activities should be supervised at all times by an adult. Any material, food, or toy given to a young child should be reviewed for safety.

Problem Solving

Activities to Help Your Baby Grow and Learn

Your newborn baby can do amazing things. Your baby can see your face when you hold her close. She can hear your voice. She can hold your finger in her hand. Your baby's brain is growing very fast, and play is very important for her brain development. Right now play is about interacting with you and very simple objects or toys. In the first months, your baby can only see things that are about 8–10 inches away; everything else is fuzzy. Your baby's brain is taking in sounds she hears from the very beginning. Very soon she will begin to under-stand simple words.

Circles and Waves	You can make a simple picture for your baby to look at. Use a piece of cardboard and nontoxic black or red markers. Draw thick, simple, large lines with curves or circles. To help him focus, bring it close (about 10 inches). Wow. That is cool!
Rattles and Rainbows	When your baby is lying on her back, hold an object about 10 inches above her head. A rattle that makes a little noise will help get her attention. Slowly move the object back and forth in a rainbow arch from side to side. You can also make a rainbow from her belly to above her fore-head. Your baby will watch the object with her eyes.
Look at Me!	Hold your baby close to your face. Smile, stick out your tongue, or make a silly face. Do this slowly so baby can take it all in. Watch what he does!
Simple Stories	At quiet times and before sleep, talk to your baby in a soft, gentle voice. Tell her simple stories or talk about the day. She will not understand you at first, but she will very soon. What she will love is being cuddled and looked at and listening to your voice.
Sing to Me	Baby will love to hear your high, sing-songy voice. Talk slowly in a high voice. You do not have to talk "baby talk." You can look at a picture book and talk about the pictures. Or just talk! He will soon begin to make sounds to talk to you.
Lap Time	After a few weeks, your baby can hold her head up while you hold her in your lap. Put new things close to her to look at on the floor or the table. She will enjoy seeing these things up close. Tell your baby what she is seeing: "Cup. That's your cup." "Look, here is your sock."

Notes:

 Don't Forget! Activities should be supervised at all times by an adult. Any material, food, or toy given to a young child should be reviewed for safety.

Personal-Social
Activities to Help Your Baby Grow and Learn

Your new baby needs you right now. She depends on you to feed her and keep her warm and safe. Your baby interacts by looking at you or using her voice to get your attention. When you respond to her cries, she learns to trust you. She will enjoy being held and talked to by others in the family, but you are the most important person in your baby's world.

Mealtime Moments	As baby nurses or takes a bottle, softly touch her little cheek, forehead, or tiny ears. Look her in the eyes and tell her she is like no other—your own little miracle. Your baby may want to stay right there in your arms, even if she is not eating.
What Did You Say?	As soon as your baby is born, he is trying to tell you something. Babies' first "words" are cries that say, "I want you," "I'm cold," "I'm hungry," or "I'm tired." Listen and learn what each cry means. Talk to him: "Are you hungry?" "Are you tired, little baby?"
Whose Hand Is That?	When your baby is rested and not hungry, place her on her back and sit next to her. Stay close. Tell her you love her. Talk to baby about her body: "Look at your hands! Your fingers!" Everything is new and interesting to her. Even her body parts are amazing!
Smiley Face	Smile at your baby all day, especially when diapering, bathing, or feeding your baby. Give him little nose kisses. In the first few weeks, your baby's smile is mostly a reflex, but soon he will smile back at you. What a wonderful sight!
What's Next?	Talk to your baby about her day and what is going to happen next. She does not know the words yet but will very soon. This will help your baby learn the routine: "It's time for a nap." "It's time to eat."
Give Me a Break!	Your wonderful baby is able to let you know he needs a break. He may do things like look away, yawn, cry, or arch his back. He may need a nap or just a little break. After a rest, he will be ready to enjoy his interesting world again.

Notes:

 Don't Forget! Activities should be supervised at all times by an adult. Any material, food, or toy given to a young child should be reviewed for safety.

Communication

Activities to Help Your Baby Grow and Learn

2–4 months

Your wonderful new person communicates with her whole body. Her gaze tells you that you are the most important person in the world. She communicates with body movements, noises, and her own special cry when she needs something. Your baby's favorite music is your gentle voice. Even though your baby enjoys the sounds of a busy household, some quiet time is important so that she can hear family voices.

Musical Moments	Sing as you bathe, feed, exercise, or change your baby. Introduce favorite tunes and rhymes, or make up your own. Add baby's name now and then. "Twinkle, twinkle, little Andie. How I love my little Andie." Let your baby watch your face. Baby knows how important she is!
Funny Baby	During quiet and happy times, encourage your baby to smile. Make funny (not scary) faces that he likes. When baby smiles, be sure to make that face again. Tell baby how funny he is!
Picture Books	With your baby cuddled on your lap, hold a book with simple, clear, colorful pictures so that both of you can see. You could also look at magazine pictures, newspaper food advertisements, or family photos. Talk softly about what you see as you point to the pictures. Baby will learn that reading time is very special.
Special Talking Time	When your baby is awake, cuddle her and hold her so she can see your face. Talk for a little while. Look at her face as she looks at yours. Encourage her to make different sounds, coos, and squeals. Have a conversation.
Words for Baby's Cry	As you comfort baby when he cries, talk about why he is crying. Try to figure out what is wrong, and tell him about it as you take care of his needs.
Noticing Sounds	When sounds happen around the house, help baby notice by talking about them: "I hear the phone ringing. I hear your brother calling."
Phone Time	When talking on the phone, hold your baby close and look at her. Baby will enjoy watching and listening to you. She'll think your conversation is just for her!

Notes:

(👆) **Don't Forget!** Activities should be supervised at all times by an adult. Any material, food, or toy given to a young child should be reviewed for safety. Always stay with baby during bath time.

Gross Motor

Activities to Help Your Baby Grow and Learn

2–4 months

Baby is gaining strength right from the beginning. He practices lifting and controlling his head. He moves his arms and legs. Soon he will be able to roll from his back to his side. He likes being held so that his feet gently touch a surface. He likes to be held in a sitting position so that he can strengthen his back and tummy muscles and see what's going on.

Position Changes	When baby is awake, place baby in different positions, such as on her stomach or side. This will allow baby to move her arms and legs in different ways or directions. This also will strengthen baby's body and make her view more interesting.
Kicking Practice	Place baby on his back on a firm surface. As you talk quietly to baby, encourage him to move his legs. Hold a foot in each hand and gently move his feet back and forth.
Heads Up	Put baby on her stomach. Dangle a bright toy in front of her, or make faces and sounds to encourage your baby to lift her head. Then give her a big smile. While you walk with your baby's head by your shoulder, pass by a bright curtain or picture. Give her time to lift her head and look: "Wow, little one, look at that! Your neck is so strong!"
Bath Time for Two	One special way to bathe baby is with you. Enjoy gently massaging his legs, arms, tummy, and back. Allow baby to kick and splash as you hold him safely and talk and sing a little bath time song.
Balancing Act *(about 3–4 months)*	Stand baby on your knees. With your hands around her little body, gently hold her in a standing position. Let her support as much of her own weight as she can to help her strengthen her legs and gain balance. Hold her so she looks at you, and then smile. Next time hold her so she's looking out. There's so much to see!
Roll Over	Encourage baby to roll from his stomach to his back by holding a bright toy in front of him and slowly moving it over to the side. You may need to help him roll over with your hand until he can do it himself.
Pretty Pull-Ups *(about 3–4 months)*	Place baby on your lap facing you. Pull her up slowly by her arms. Then, gently lower her in an up-and-down game. Talk to her as she moves up and down. This will help to strengthen stomach muscles and let baby see the world and your smiling face from a different point of view.

Notes:

Don't Forget! Activities should be supervised at all times by an adult. Any material, food, or toy given to a young child should be reviewed for safety. Always watch baby when she is on her stomach or in water.

Fine Motor
Activities to Help Your Baby Grow and Learn

Your baby is gaining control of her gaze and can focus on a nearby object for a few seconds. Soon she'll be able to follow you with her eyes while you move around. Her fist will grasp your finger and hold on tightly. She will show excitement by waving her arms. She is beginning to notice what's going on in the world; what a wonderful time!

Finger Kiss	When feeding baby, encourage him to touch your lips (if he doesn't do this spontaneously). Kiss his fingertips. Baby will learn the soft, wet sensation of your lips and soon will learn to aim his fingers toward your lips.
Gotcha *(about 3–4 months)*	While your baby is lying on a firm surface or sitting so that she faces you, offer a toy or something to grasp just beyond her reach. When she reaches for it, make sure she gets it. She'll probably taste it, too!
Finger Grip	Let your baby grab your finger and grip it tightly. Gently tug a little just to let your baby know you're there: "My, you are so strong!"
Finger and Toe Rub	Rub your baby's fingers and toes one at a time. A little oil or baby lotion makes this especially nice. Your baby will enjoy the way it feels. It will also help baby learn about his body. Talk softly as you rub him: "I love your beautiful little toes."
Ribbon Flutter	Hang a long, brightly colored ribbon or scarf loosely around your neck. When you lean over to change baby or pick her up, let her reach out and touch the ribbon. Talk about what she is doing: "You touched the pretty ribbon. I wore it just for you!"
Tuggy Tuggy Tug	Let baby grasp a dishcloth or the corner of a washcloth. Slightly tug the other end. Tell him how strong he is. Let go gently and let him win the pulling game!

Notes:

Don't Forget! Activities should be supervised at all times by an adult. Any material, food, or toy given to a young child should be reviewed for safety.

Problem Solving
Activities to Help Your Baby Grow and Learn

Your baby already responds to sounds and voices. He's beginning to look for the source of the noise. He also looks at his surroundings and will show an active interest in a person or toy. He likes to study things, such as his own hands and his favorite face—yours!

Tracking Fun	Let baby follow a rattle, a shiny spoon, or your face with his eyes. Hold your face or an object 10–12 inches from baby's face and slowly move from left to right. Talk softly as you play. Baby will enjoy being part of the action.
Light Touch	Stroke your baby gently with a feather, a cotton ball, or the edge of a cloth. Your baby will enjoy the sensation as she learns to find and feel different body parts. Talk to baby softly. Describe what she is feeling.
Cotton Ball Sniff	To help your baby develop his sense of smell, put a bit of toothpaste on your finger, or hold a sweet smelling bar of soap. If you have them in your kitchen, you might put a drop of mint or vanilla on a tissue or cotton ball. Gently wave these smells near baby so he can experience the scent: "Mmm, it smells so good."
Making Faces	With baby on her back, lean over her and make surprised or happy faces. Encourage her to reach for your nose or lips or mouth. Have a little laugh together.
Colorful Socks	Put brightly colored socks on your baby's feet. This will encourage him to look at his feet and start to reach for them! This game will help baby discover parts of his own body: "Wow, look at those pretty feet!"
Spoon Sounds	Lay your baby on her back and dangle a couple of shiny spoons above her so she can reach and bat them: "Listen. Did you hear them tinkling?" Shiny spoons also make a nice hanging crib toy to entertain baby as long as they are safely out of reach.
Reaching Practice *(about 3–4 months)*	Place baby in your lap or the lap of another special person. Hold up a safe and interesting toy for baby to reach for. Let baby be successful by slowly moving the toy to his fingers: "You got it!"

Notes:

Don't Forget! Activities should be supervised at all times by an adult. Any material, food, or toy given to a young child should be reviewed for safety.

Personal-Social
Activities to Help Your Baby Grow and Learn

2–4 months

Baby will look into your eyes to tell you, "I'm yours." She loves and needs a lot of holding and physical contact. When she needs you, she will fuss or cry. Your response and gentle voice will comfort her. When she is taking in information, she will be calmer. This is often after eating, resting, or having a diaper changed. She is now able to smile at happy faces that please her, mostly yours!

Love and Trust Building	Respond right away when baby cries. It's her way of telling you something important. Carry, hug, smile, sing, and talk to baby often. It's your way of saying, "I love you, and I'll take care of you."
Communicating Through Touch	After his bath, baby may be ready for a massage. Use baby oil and gently massage his arms, hands, legs, feet, back, tummy, and bottom. Continue only as long as your baby is quiet and content. Talk or sing a little song. You can make it up—baby won't mind.
Funny Face Play	Make an *oh* face; slowly stick out your tongue or pucker your lips when baby seems to be studying your face. Hold that expression and see if your baby will imitate it. Smile if baby copies you!
Looking in the Mirror	Hold your baby up in front of a mirror. She may enjoy smiling and making noises at herself. As baby looks in the mirror, she is learning about your gentle touch and about the "other baby" she sees.
Peekaboo	Play Peekaboo with your baby. Place your hands over your eyes. Release your hands and say, "Boo." Place a blanket over your head then drop the blanket and say, "Boo!" Your baby will enjoy many variations of this game for a long time to come.
Firm Grip	As baby's fist begins to relax, place a small toy in his hand. He won't be very good at letting go just yet. Let him grasp your finger while he nurses. Smile and tell him how strong he is!

Notes:

Don't Forget! Activities should be supervised at all times by an adult. Any material, food, or toy given to a young child should be reviewed for safety.

ASQ-3™ Learning Activities by Elizabeth Twombly and Ginger Fink.
Copyright © 2013 by Paul H. Brookes Publishing Co. All rights reserved.

19

Communication

Activities to Help Your Baby Grow and Learn

Your baby knows his name and may use his voice to let you know he is happy. He can shout for your attention. He squeals and is beginning to babble to you and to others. He makes sounds such as "mama" or "dada." He also is learning to respond to "bye-bye."

Baby Rubdown	After bath time, enjoy some quiet time talking with your baby as you gently rub him down with lotion or oil. Tell him about your day and ask about his: "We went to the market today. You wore your new shirt from Grandma."
What's That?	When your baby notices a sound, help her locate the source. Ask your baby questions: "What's that? Daddy's car? Did you hear a dog?"
Touch that Sound	As your baby begins to experiment with his voice at about 5 months, you will probably hear "ba," "mmm," and "da" and "ah," "ee," and "oo" sounds. Imitate the sounds baby makes. While you make the sound, let your baby put his fingers on your lips to feel the vibrations.
Trust Building with Words	When you move away from your baby to do other things, keep in touch with your baby through your words. Tell her what you are doing as she follows with her eyes: "I'm over here. I'm picking up the clothes. I'll be right back." Now and then step out of sight but continue to talk until you return: "Did you miss me?"
Reading Time	Your baby will enjoy looking at pictures in magazines or books. Choose things such as a phone, dog, car, or spoon. Sit with your baby on your lap and read or talk about the pictures. Tell a little story: "See the phone? It's for you."
Sing a Song	When you are bathing, diapering, or changing your baby's clothes, sing a song: "This is the way we wash our toes, wash our toes, wash our toes. This is the way we wash our toes, so early in the morning."
Hide and Seek	Move just out of sight and call baby's name. Wait a few seconds and then reappear: "Here I am!" Now find another place and hide again.

Notes:

Don't Forget! Activities should be supervised at all times by an adult. Any material, food, or toy given to a young child should be reviewed for safety. Always watch baby when he is in water.

21

Gross Motor

Activities to Help Your Baby Grow and Learn

Your baby gets stronger every minute. She now holds her head up and looks all around at everything that's going on. She is learning to sit by herself, even though at first she uses her hands for support. She loves standing while you hold her. Soon she will be able to pull herself up.

Floor Time	Spread out a quilt on the floor or outside in a shaded spot. Put your baby on the blanket on her tummy with a few of her favorite toys and encourage her to stretch, scoot, roll, squirm, or wiggle her way to the toys. Be sure to give some time for baby to be on her back, too.
Sitting Pretty	Help your baby sit alone. Sit behind him and give him some gentle support. A big sister or brother could also do this. At first, baby might want to help hold himself up with his hands. Later baby can hold a toy or a book. Whisper in his ear that he is a wonderful baby! As he learns to sit by himself, you can give him less help.
Bouncy Baby	Hold on to your baby's hands and help her stand up. Have fun bouncing up and down while she's standing on the floor, the sofa, or your lap. Sing a little bouncing chant: "Bouncy, bouncy, bouncy, stop." What fun!
Stand-Up Play *(about 7 months)*	Your baby may enjoy standing up while holding on to tables and chairs and reaching for different objects. Remove breakable items from low tables or shelves, and line up some of his favorite toys to reach for.
Little Explorer	Now that baby is learning to crawl, she'll want to explore the whole house: "What's under the table? What's behind the chair?" Make sure the areas where she can explore are safe and clean. What good exercise for both of you!
Obstacle Course *(about 6–7 months)*	Once your baby has started to crawl, you can make a simple obstacle course of pillows and blankets for your baby to crawl across and around.
Kitchen Helper	As your baby gets better at sitting alone, give your baby a small pan or pot lid and a spoon to play with. Baby will enjoy the noise as he bangs it, pats it, and rolls it.

Notes:

 Don't Forget! Activities should be supervised at all times by an adult. Any material, food, or toy given to a young child should be reviewed for safety. Always watch closely when baby is on her tummy.

ASQ-3™ Learning Activities by Elizabeth Twombly and Ginger Fink.
Copyright © 2013 by Paul H. Brookes Publishing Co. All rights reserved.

Fine Motor
Activities to Help Your Baby Grow and Learn

4–8 months

Your baby's grasp has relaxed now, and he likes to reach and grab nearby objects. He can hold and bang objects and even hold something in each hand! He may watch you scribble with interest. He's learning how to use his fingers and is getting better at it every day.

Rattles and Toys	Give your baby plenty of opportunities to try out different toys. Things that feel different or toys that make sounds will be very interesting to your baby. Some of the best toys aren't toys at all, such as spoons.
Picky, Picky *(6 months or older)*	When your baby starts eating solid food, he will enjoy trying to pick up small bits with his thumb and forefinger. Don't worry about the mess. This fun activity strengthens eyes and fingers.
Ice Is Nice	Crush ice into very small pieces that baby can safely eat. Your baby will love to explore the cold ice as it squirms around in a bowl. The crushed ice and cool fingers will feel good on baby's gums and new little teeth!
Drop and Dump	As soon as your baby can sit alone, she can sit on the floor and play some dropping games. Use a plastic container and a small ball, block, or toy. Let your baby drop the ball into the container. You may need to help her at first. Now dump it out. She will want to try it again and again!
Finger Paint	Put a dab of soft, smooth food (e.g., yogurt, soft mashed carrots) on a plate or cookie sheet and let your baby "paint" with her fingers. It's all right if he eats the "paint."
Noodle Pull	Give baby a serving of cool, cooked noodles. Let baby pull apart a few strands. This is a fun way to practice using fingers and to snack at the same time.
Cereal Spill	Put a few pieces of round dry cereal in a plastic bottle. See if your baby can figure out how to tip over the bottle to feed herself the cereal.
Busy Bath Time	Make bath time fun. This is a good time to practice holding and pouring. Add plastic cups and a plastic pitcher to baby's bath. What wet, bubbly fun!

Notes:

 Don't Forget! Activities should be supervised at all times by an adult. Any material, food, or toy given to a young child should be reviewed for safety. Remember—never leave baby alone in water and always watch while baby eats.

ASQ-3™ Learning Activities by Elizabeth Twombly and Ginger Fink. | 25
Copyright © 2013 by Paul H. Brookes Publishing Co. All rights reserved.

Problem Solving

Activities to Help Your Baby Grow and Learn

4–8 months

Your busy learner is interested in making things work! She will find a toy that's partly hidden and will reach with all her might for something that's just out of reach. She knows when a voice is friendly or angry and much prefers friendly sounds. She also loves playing hiding games, such as Peekaboo!

Where Did It Go?	Move your face or a favorite toy behind a cover while your baby is watching. Ask, "Where is Mommy?" Drop the cover and say, "Here I am!" Cover baby's doll or bear. Ask, "Where is the bear?" Move the cloth and say, "There he is!"
Bath Time Boats	Put several plastic containers in your baby's bath. She will delight in learning about sinking, floating, dumping, and pouring.
Reactions	Provide baby with toys that react such as squeak toys, pull toys, and pop-up toys. Let baby discover ways to make things happen! Share baby's surprise: "Look what happened!"
Hide a Squeak Toy	Hide a toy or some item that makes noise, such as a bell or set of measuring spoons, under a blanket while your baby watches. Reach under the blanket and make the sound. Let him try to find it. Now hide the toy to the side, then behind your baby. Let him look around, then "help" him find it!
Music Maker	Give baby a spoon or a block for each hand. Show her how to bang them on a tabletop or highchair tray while you sing a song. Sing and tap loudly, then sing and tap very softly. Hooray for the band!
Hide the Baby	This is a fun version of Peekaboo. While folding laundry or doing the dishes, cover baby with a sheet, towel, or dishcloth. Say, "'Where's the baby?" Wait a second and pull down the cloth. "Surprise! There's the baby!"
Safe Sandbox	In a small container or tray, let baby touch some flour. As you do this, talk about how it feels and show him how to sift it through his fingers: "Ooh, that's so soft."

Notes:

Don't Forget! Activities should be supervised at all times by an adult. Any material, food, or toy given to a young child should be reviewed for safety. Always watch baby when she is in water.

27

Personal-Social

Activities to Help Your Baby Grow and Learn

Your baby knows you very well now and will lift his arms to come to you. He may begin to fret when strangers approach. He likes to play with his image in the mirror and is really quite sociable as long as he feels safe and secure.

A Cup for Baby	Allow your baby to hold a plastic cup. Put a little water in it and see what baby will do. She will probably enjoy trying to drink out of a cup. Let her experiment. A bib is a good idea. (You might also want to have a small towel handy!)
Body Awareness	Your baby is discovering different body parts and probably has become very interested in his feet and hands. Encourage him by playing games with fingers and toes, such as "This Little Piggy." Talk about his body parts. When he touches his feet, say, "You found your feet!"
Self-Feeding	Encourage your baby to pick up and eat safe foods, such as crackers or cereal bits. You may also give baby her own spoon to hold while you feed her with another spoon. Try taking turns— you pretend to eat a little and then offer a bite to your baby. Baby will understand that feeding herself is the way to go.
Whisper Power	Rock, walk, or dance and whisper sweet words in your baby's ear. Whispering to your baby helps him to calm down and provides another way to talk in a quiet and loving voice.
A Social Hour	Invite another parent and baby over to play with your baby. As the babies look at, reach for, and explore each other, they will make important discoveries about real people. Stay close by to keep each baby safe as they do their exploring.
Wave Bye-Bye	Wave bye-bye when you leave the room for a moment or two. As you wave, tell your baby where you are going: "I am going into your bedroom to get your blanket. I'll be right back. Bye-bye."
Faces in the Mirror	While looking in the mirror with your baby, talk about body parts, such as the eyes, nose, and ears. Touch your nose and say, "Daddy's nose!" Touch baby's nose and say, "Baby's nose." Then say, "Daddy's eyes, baby's eyes." Play this game as long as baby seems interested.

Notes:

 Don't Forget! Activities should be supervised at all times by an adult. Any material, food, or toy given to a young child should be reviewed for safety. Always watch baby while she is eating.

Communication

Activities to Help Your Baby Grow and Learn

Your baby now has many different sounds and a lot to say. She likes to play with sounds, such as "ba ba ba," and is learning that some sounds mean special people, such as "dada" and "papa." She understands some words and directions now and will soon say the names of familiar people or things.

Following Directions
Help your baby learn to listen and follow simple directions. Try simple directions, such as "Show me Grandma," "Wash your tummy," or "Hold the diaper." When baby responds or follows the direction, be sure to let him know you notice: "Oh, there's Grandma" or "Thank you for holding the diaper."

Grocery Time Is Learning Time
When you go to the food market, talk to baby about what she is seeing. Let her hold a small box or a piece of fruit. Point out signs in the store and read them to your baby: "That sign says *apples*. Let's get some nice red apples."

The Phone Game
Talk to your baby on a play phone or an old cell phone. Be sure to remove the battery before giving it to baby. When there are two phones, you can both "talk," even though baby may only make her baby sounds or pretend to listen. Your baby will have fun carrying on a conversation just like big people.

Sleep Waltz
At naptime or bedtime, hold your baby close and dance together to some quiet music. Your baby has probably spent a lot of time exploring during the day. Now she needs some cuddling. This communicates to baby a feeling of closeness and intimacy.

Just My Voice
When baby is awake and alert, turn off the television and other household sounds so that he only hears your voice. This helps baby hear the sounds of words more clearly. Hum and sing just for baby's pleasure. Ask baby, "Can you hear a bird? Can you hear the rain?"

Baby Babble Game
When your baby makes a sound, such as "ba," repeat the sound back: "Ba ba ba." Your baby will enjoy playing with sounds and making conversation.

Applause, Applause
When baby does something new or fun, give baby a hand. Clap and say, "Yeah!" Baby will love the attention and may start to clap, too!

Reading Fun
Read to your baby every day. Cuddle up, get close, and make this a special time together. Point to pictures in books or ask her to find something: "Where's the kitty? Where are baby's socks?"

Notes:

 Don't Forget! Activities should be supervised at all times by an adult. Any material, food, or toy given to a young child should be reviewed for safety.

Gross Motor

Activities to Help Your Baby Grow and Learn

This is a very active period for your baby. He's now pulling up on furniture, crawling and creeping into places he couldn't reach before, and getting ready to walk. In fact, he will probably walk holding on to your hand and attempt a few steps without your help. Baby is on the move!

Money in the Bank

Save large lids from jars to use as "money." Now that your baby can sit on her own, let her put these round things into a clean container. Then shake the container and make a great noise. Dump them out and put the "money" in the bank again.

Kick, Kick

When you are changing your baby's diaper or getting him ready for bed, play this game. As your baby kicks his legs, sing in rhythm to the kicking. When your baby stops kicking, stop singing. When he starts again, start singing. This will develop into a fun game of stop and go. Your baby not only exercises his muscles, but he gets to be the boss.

Reaching for Fun

If your baby is pulling herself to a standing position, put some of her favorite toys on a low table and let her stretch way out to reach them. This will give her practice with reaching and balancing. She will also be learning about ideas such as near and far.

Rain, Rain in the Tub

Get a small empty plastic container, put some holes in it, and let your baby fill it with water during bath time. Help him to hold it up and discover "rain" for himself while you supervise.

Walking Practice

Once your baby has started to walk, she will want to practice a lot. Show her how to hold on to a lightweight but stable chair or stool and push it around the room. Sturdy cardboard boxes also make great push toys. Let your baby push things indoors and outside.

Tunneling

While folding laundry, throw a blanket or sheet over a table or the backs of two chairs. Let your little explorer crawl into the "tunnel." When he's out of sight, call him. Then, greet him with surprise when he finds you: "Oh, there you are!"

Notes:

Don't Forget! Activities should be supervised at all times by an adult. Any material, food, or toy given to a young child should be reviewed for safety. Always stay with baby when he is in water.

Fine Motor

Activities to Help Your Baby Grow and Learn

Your busy baby is beginning to pick up tiny bits of food with her thumb and forefinger. She can take things out of a container, such as spoons out of a plastic bowl, and can bang two toys together. If you give her a crayon and paper, she may even attempt to imitate your writing with a scribble.

Feely Game	In a cardboard box, collect things to feel, hold, and bang. Good items might include an empty plastic bottle, a toothbrush, and a little shoe. Let baby reach into the box to grab something and pull it out to show you. Talk about what he is holding. This exercise for little muscles also helps baby explore how different things feel.
Find the Feet	With baby sitting on the floor or the bed, drop a towel or small blanket over baby's feet. Ask baby, "Where are your feet?" Let baby pull off the blanket and show you her feet: "Hooray! There they are." Then play it again!
Catcher's Up	Use a small, soft ball (or make a ball out of socks rolled together) and play catch with your baby. He won't be able to really catch the ball yet, but he will enjoy trying to throw it and chase after it.
Tearing	Get a big basket or box and put some old magazines and wrapping paper inside. Let your baby tear what she wants. If she is more interested in putting wads of paper in her mouth, put the box away and try again in a few weeks.
Sticks and Stones	Take a walk outside. Encourage your baby to pick up items, such as stones, twigs, and leaves. Put them in a pail or paper bag. Talk about the color or the size: "Look, this big leaf is nice!"
Goodies in a Jar	Put small pieces of cereal in a screw-top or snap-top plastic container. Put the lid on loosely. Let baby take the lid off. You may have to show your baby how to take the lid off and get the cereal. Soon he will do it by himself.
Bedtime Book Time	A great way to get ready for bed is to snuggle up and read books with your baby. Let her pick a few books and help turn the pages. Talk about the pictures and ask her to point to things she sees. Enjoy your special time.

Notes:

Don't Forget! Activities should be supervised at all times by an adult. Any material, food, or toy given to a young child should be reviewed for safety. Remember to watch out for things that might go into your baby's mouth.

 ASQ-3™ Learning Activities by Elizabeth Twombly and Ginger Fink. Copyright © 2013 by Paul H. Brookes Publishing Co. All rights reserved.

Problem Solving

Activities to Help Your Baby Grow and Learn

As baby learns how things work, he will be busy taking them apart. He can take pieces out of a puzzle or rings off a stack. He is learning how to find hidden objects under a blanket. He enjoys looking at pictures in a book and enjoys when you name the pictures. He's been so busy exploring that he probably now knows the word *no*.

Rhythm Play	Give your baby spoons to drum on a table or a pot. Clap blocks or sticks together to make sounds. Sing along and dance a little. Enjoy the music!
Scarf Play	Tie several colorful scarves together. Insert one end into a cardboard tube. Let your baby pull the scarves through the tube. Now see if your baby can stuff the scarves back into the tube.
Listen and Find	Hide a ticking clock or a toy that makes sounds under a pillow or blanket. Let your baby listen to find the sound: "Do you hear it? Where is it? Can you find it?"
A Third Toy	Give your baby a toy or object when she is holding something in each hand. See if she can figure out a way to take the third item and hold on to all three. If this is too difficult for your baby right now, try it again in a few weeks.
In and Out	Put a piece of cereal inside a clear plastic container or bottle without a lid. As your baby works to get the cereal out, he will learn more about inside and outside. Another way to show baby *inside* and *outside* is to get a big box that your baby can crawl into and out of.
Little Laughs *(about 11 months)*	Your baby is beginning to develop a sense of humor. Do something funny, such as trying to put baby's sock on your foot or putting a clean pair of pants on your head. She just might giggle or laugh out loud! Funny Mommy! Silly Daddy!
Lift the Cup	Place a cup and a small toy on a tray for baby. Hide the toy under the cup and ask, "Where is the toy?" If he doesn't find it, lift the cup and show your baby where it is. Say, "You found it!" Do this several times. Soon he will lift the cup and find the toy all by himself. Later, add another cup. See if baby can remember which cup hides the toy.

Notes:

Don't Forget! Activities should be supervised at all times by an adult. Any material, food, or toy given to a young child should be reviewed for safety.

Personal-Social

Activities to Help Your Baby Grow and Learn

Your baby may fear strangers and want only you. She loves to explore her environment and needs your watchful eye to keep her safe. She knows her likes and dislikes and shows love for you and even favorite toys. She can help you dress her by holding up a foot for a sock or pushing her arm into a sleeve, but she is not ready to dress herself independently.

Bath-Time Helper

When your baby is taking a bath, give her the washcloth. Encourage her to wash by herself. After the bath, let your baby help herself get dressed by pushing her arm through her nightshirt. Be patient; these self-help skills take a lot of time and practice. Be sure to give her lots of praise: "What a good job you did getting dressed!"

Follow Me

Your baby is learning to enjoy imitation. Encourage this by showing your baby how to play Follow the Leader. Use simple movements, such as tapping on the table or putting a hat on your head. Talk about what you are doing. Say, "It's your turn," and see if your baby will follow along. Let your baby have a turn at being the leader.

Party Time

Your baby may enjoy watching older children play, especially when he has older brothers or sisters. If there are other babies his age in the neighborhood, he will enjoy playing alongside them. At first, they will enjoy watching each other. Eventually, they will learn to play together.

Little Helper

Give your baby a damp sponge. Let her wipe the table, chairs, floor, walls, and doors—whatever she can reach. She may enjoy doing this while you are getting dinner ready or washing dishes. Baby won't really clean anything but will feel proud of doing things "just like mommy." Tell baby, "Thank you for helping Mommy (or Daddy)."

Snack Time

Your baby will enjoy feeding himself during snack time. Give him a few choices of simple foods such as crackers, pieces of fruit, or bits of cereal. He'll even enjoy trying to drink out of an open cup with a little help.

Mirror, Mirror

When you have a moment at home or while running errands, stop and encourage your baby to look at her face in a mirror. Make silly faces. Tell her what a big girl she is getting to be!

Roly-Poly Game

While sitting on the floor, roll a small ball to baby, and then ask him to roll it back. Now do it again. Then do it just a little faster! This is a fun game to play with an older sister or brother.

Notes:

Don't Forget! Activities should be supervised at all times by an adult. Any material, food, or toy given to a young child should be reviewed for safety. Remember to always supervise baby during bath time and mealtime.

Communication

Activities to Help Your Baby Grow and Learn

12–16 months

Your baby's babbling is beginning to sound more like talking. He says "mama" and really means it. He also is beginning to learn the names of things. He may say "no" if he is not happy. Because he's so busy learning to walk, his language use may slow down a bit. He may combine a word with pointing or using his hand to gesture, but you know very well what he means.

Hide the Noises
Show your baby two things that make noise, such as a squeak toy, a set of measuring spoons, keys on a ring, or a rattle. Let baby play with them for a while, then hide the items under a box or cloth and make a noise with one. Take the cloth off and ask baby, "Which one made the noise?" See if she can guess.

Quiet Time
On weekends or at a time that's not busy, spend time with baby in a quiet place with no music and no television (perhaps outside). Talk to your baby about what you're doing or about what baby is doing. Let your baby hear your voice and see your face making words. Talk calmly and tell baby how special he is. When your baby talks, encourage him. Have a conversation.

Rhythm Clapping
While listening to music, show baby how to move and clap in rhythm. Your baby will enjoy moving to the beat. Play different types of music, such as rock, country, hip-hop, funk, electronic, pop, or classical. Be sure to keep the volume down. Those sweet ears have to last a long time!

Listening on the Phone
When Uncle or Grandpa calls, ask him to spend a few minutes talking to baby. Baby probably won't talk back yet, but she will be delighted to hear someone's voice coming through the phone.

Big Talk
While you do housework or get a meal together, talk to your baby about what you are doing. Encourage your little one to use two words together to make baby sentences, such as "Help me" or "More juice." This big language step will grow into a lot of talk.

Little Reader
Read to your baby every day. Snuggle up and make this a special time. Point to pictures and name things for her. Sometimes ask her to find something: "Where's the cat? Oh, here it is." She may need a little help from you at first.

Big Helper
Your baby can be a big helper. Give him simple directions: "Can you get me a napkin?" or "Give me your shirt, please." He may need you to point or help a little. Say, "What a big help. Thanks!"

Notes:

Gross Motor

Activities to Help Your Baby Grow and Learn

By now your busy baby can move around the house quickly. She may be standing by herself, walking while holding onto furniture, or walking well on her own. She will try to climb up steps, so your watchful eye is very important. Baby loves to push and pull things and is getting stronger every day.

Let's Go for a Walk	Your baby will love going for walks and seeing new things. Talk to her about what you are seeing. In an open area, let baby push her own stroller. She will enjoy the feeling of power as she moves something big all by herself. Be sure to watch that she keeps the stroller where it is safe.
Row the Boat	Let your child experience rocking on a rocking horse or in a chair. Sit him on your lap and use your body to rock back and forth. Play with him sitting opposite you on the floor. Hold hands and gently pull and push him to and from you. Sing a little song, such as "Row, Row, Row Your Boat," while you rock back and forth.
Moving Day	Give your baby a box large enough to push while standing. Show her how to fill it with a few toys, small cartons, or boxes. Let her push these things around the room from one area to another. She may want to take everything out. If so, show her how to put it all back in again!
Have a Ball	Your baby will enjoy playing with balls. You can sit across from him and roll a ball to him. Encourage him to roll it back. Clap your hands when he does. If the ball is big and soft (e.g., beach ball with some of the air out), he may be able to "catch" it by stopping it when it gets to him.
Finger Walk	Take a little walk with baby holding on to your finger. Baby can choose to hold on or to let go. Talk to baby about what you see and where you're going: "Let's walk over to those plants. Let's walk down the hall. You're a good walker!"
Dance Party	Play some fun dancing music and show baby how to dance! Wiggle and turn, clap, and stomp your feet. Try lots of different kinds of music. Wave around some scarves and ribbons. Get other family members to join in. Have a dance party.

Notes:

Fine Motor

Activities to Help Your Baby Grow and Learn

12–16 months

Baby is using fingers with more skill now. He will point with his index finger and can pick up tiny bits of cereal with his thumb and finger. He can hold and mark with a crayon or washable marker and grasp small objects, such small blocks or other small toys.

Budding Artist	Let baby draw a picture for you with a crayon and a large piece of paper. Give baby plenty of room. She may only make a few marks, but give a lot of praise: "Look at the picture you made!" Be sure to put the crayon away when you are finished. Your baby doesn't yet know that you only want marks on the paper.
Ball Toss	Encourage your baby to practice throwing a small, soft ball. A rolled up pair of socks works just fine. Have him stand in one spot and throw the ball. Try again and see how far it goes. At first, he may need you to show him how to throw the ball. Say, "Wow, look how far it went!"
Carton Construction	Save different sizes of paper cereal boxes or juice boxes to use for blocks. Show baby how to stack them, then knock them down. Line them up to make a wall and then knock them down again: "What fun to knock them all down!"
Tacky Tape	Make a small wad of masking tape with the sticky side out. Give this to baby to play with. It is very entertaining and will give baby some good finger exercise.
Squeezing	Give baby a sponge, washcloth, or sponge ball to play with in the bath. Show baby how to squeeze the water out. You might also let baby play with plastic squirt toys. That's really fun!
Fill and Dump	Give baby a container or box and a few items such as clothespins, spoons, and small cars. Make sure the items are big enough that they can't be swallowed. Show baby how to put them all in the container, then dump them out again. The next day, change the container or the objects. Make this activity a bit more challenging by choosing a container with a smaller opening.
Library Time	Find a time every 2 weeks or so to go to a library or bookstore. Pick out new books with your child. Cuddle every day and read together. Read the story, talk about pictures, and let her take turns pointing to pictures and turning pages. What a special time together!

Notes:

Don't Forget! Activities should be supervised at all times by an adult. Any material, food, or toy given to a young child should be reviewed for safety. Always watch baby during bath time.

Problem Solving

Activities to Help Your Baby Grow and Learn

Your baby is a busy explorer. She enjoys holding, stacking, and playing with toys. She is learning her body parts and can probably point to at least one if you ask her. She enjoys books and will "pat" her favorite picture. She may try to help turn pages in a book. She enjoys learning about how things work.

Fill the Bank	Make a money bank out of a large can or a plastic container. Cut a long slit in the plastic cover about a half-inch wide. Cut circles from cardboard to use as "money" and show your baby how to put these "coins" into the bank.
Water Painting	Give your baby a clean paintbrush and a small bucket of plain water. On a sunny day, go outside and let your child paint the walls, sidewalk, or fence with water. Your child will enjoy this "painting." Then you can watch it dry and paint again. Try this inside with a small paintbrush and a brown paper bag. Watch the painting disappear!
Problem Solving	Let your baby figure out how things work and what they do. Show baby how the switch turns the light on and off. Show him how the flashlight works. Talk to him about what you are doing and why: "I'm putting on a coat because I am cold."
Little Hunter	During quiet times, ask your baby to find the blanket or to get a book from another room. Ask her to get things she cannot see at the time. She might need a little help. When baby is successful, be sure to say, "Thank you. You found it."
Matching Game	Children this age are just beginning to notice when two things are alike, especially shoes, socks, or other objects they know. Hold up one of baby's shoes or a sock. Ask baby, "Where's the other one just like this?" Help baby make the match: "Yes, these two are the same."
Copy Me	Play a game with your baby. You do something and then try to get baby to imitate you. Clap your hands. If he tries to imitate you, say, "Look, you can clap, too!" Touch your nose, stick out your tongue, and say, "You try." When he does something new, imitate him. Be silly and have fun.

Notes:

Don't Forget! Activities should be supervised at all times by an adult. Any material, food, or toy given to a young child should be reviewed for safety.

Personal-Social

Activities to Help Your Baby Grow and Learn

12–16 months

Your sociable baby likes to roll the ball and play Peekaboo or other games with you. He needs to know you are nearby. He actually likes to be the center of attention now! He will show you great affection but may collapse into a tantrum when things don't go his way. He is proud of his new skills, and he wants to learn how to do things by himself.

Happy Hats	Your baby may enjoy trying on different hats and looking at herself in the mirror. Make a dress-up box with a few hats. As your child gets older, you can add new things now and then.
Help Me Clean	Your baby can help do small jobs, such as wiping the table with a sponge, stirring pancake mix (with your help), or sweeping up a little dirt with a small broom. He will enjoy doing something special for you. Give him opportunities to be a helper, and let him know he is being helpful.
Brushing Teeth	Give baby her own toothbrush. Let her see you or her siblings brushing their teeth. Put a tiny dab of toothpaste (without fluoride) on the brush so baby can taste it. Don't expect much brushing. She will probably chew the bristles as she learns about this new thing, and you may need to finish for her. Be sure to cover baby's toothbrush and store it in a clean, safe place until next time.
To Market, To Market	Take baby to the supermarket with you so baby can "help." Talk about all of the colors and smells. Let baby hold something, such as a small can or a lemon. At the checkout, let baby "pay" the cashier. What a good helper!
Find Me!	At home, play Hide and Seek by hiding just behind a door, calling to baby, then peeking out so you can be found. A sibling may have fun playing this game. It helps baby understand that when you disappear, you will come back.
Bathing Baby	When bathing baby, let him bathe a small plastic doll. Show baby how to be gentle with the doll. Later, let him dry and hug the doll. It will teach him to be loving.
Cleanup Time	Ask baby to help you put the toys away. You will need a box with a safe cover or a shelf where toys should be placed. Show baby how to pick up the toys and where to put them. Keep this task easy and brief right now. It's a good idea to do it together and have fun: "What a good helper!"

Notes:

Don't Forget! Activities should be supervised at all times by an adult. Any material, food, or toy given to a young child should be reviewed for safety.

ASQ-3™ Learning Activities by Elizabeth Twombly and Ginger Fink.
Copyright © 2013 by Paul H. Brookes Publishing Co. All rights reserved.

49

Communication
Activities to Help Your Toddler Grown and Learn

Your toddler is beginning to enjoy language and words. She has many new words now and is beginning to put two words together for simple sentences. She looks at you when you are talking to her; she says "hi" and "bye," and she points to things she wants. She also enjoys singing and will try to sing her favorite songs.

Chatter Stretchers	Your toddler may use single words for requests, such as "juice" when he wants a drink. Help him stretch his sentence by saying it for him: "Would you like some juice? Say, 'I want juice, please.'" Praise him when he attempts to make the sentence longer.
What Happened Today?	When you get home from an outing, ask your toddler to tell someone else about what happened or what the two of you saw: "Tell Grandpa about the horse we saw." Help her if you need to, but let her tell as much as she can.
"Help Me" Game	Ask your toddler to help you by giving him simple directions, such as "Give Daddy his book," "Can you get my shoe?" or "Could you bring me a diaper?" You may need to point with your finger to help him in the beginning. Be sure to say, "Thank you," when he helps.
Animal Sounds	Teach your toddler the sounds that animals make. Read books about baby animals, and play with your toddler by making the baby animal sounds. Later, pretend you are the animal's parent and your toddler is the baby animal. Call each other with animal sounds. This game can be a lot of silly fun.
Read, Read, Read	Find times to "read" throughout the day. You can point to pictures and words, and your child will begin to learn what words are about. At the grocery store, point to and read signs to your child. At a restaurant, let your child "read" a menu. At home, help her "read" magazines by looking at pictures together and talking about them.
Treasure Box	Put together a treasure box of safe, everyday items that are interesting to explore and feel—plastic cups, a soft sock, a little ball, a hairbrush, a small shoe. When your child pulls something out of the box, say, "Look, you found a soft blue sock" or "That sponge is squishy." Use new language for your child, and change items in the box every few days.

Notes:

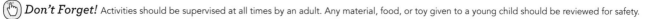 **Don't Forget!** Activities should be supervised at all times by an adult. Any material, food, or toy given to a young child should be reviewed for safety.

Gross Motor
Activities to Help Your Toddler Grow and Learn

By now, your active toddler may be attempting to run. He can carry large items and toys and loves to push and pull big things such as boxes around on the floor. He's learning how to walk upstairs with one hand held by you and is getting better at walking down stairs. He may climb up into a chair to see and reach new things. Your watchful eye is important.

Swinging	Take your child to a playground to swing. Be sure the swing is safe and has a seat belt. Show your child how to push her feet out when swinging forward. Push gently so you know she will hold on. Chant in rhythm while you push: "*Up* you go, and *up* you go!"
Climbing the Stairs	Hold your child's hand while you climb up steps or a few stairs. Be patient; stairs are very high for little legs. Don't expect much luck with climbing down just yet. If you don't have any stairs in your house or yard, a playground may have places to practice, such as a small slide or a jungle gym platform.
Balance Beam	With a strip of tape or with chalk, make a line on the floor or outside on the sidewalk. Show your child how to walk along the tape, placing one foot in front of the other. Encourage your child's new skill. Tell him, "You are learning how to balance!"
Chasing	Your toddler is beginning to run now. In a grassy part of your yard or a safe park, play chase with your little one. Most toddlers love to be chased, and they love to be caught and hugged. Your child will love doing this over and over! It's good exercise.
Wagon Pull	Give your child a small wagon or a box with a pull string for hauling toys around. Your child can load the wagon and unload at a different place. Maybe the teddy bear wants to ride!
Playing Music	Your toddler will love making and moving to music. You can make a drum with an oatmeal container, large plastic containers, and wooden spoons or chopsticks. Join her for a little music making. Take turns making music and dancing and moving to different rhythms.
Kickball	Give your child a medium-size ball (6 inches) and show him how to kick it. You can also make a ball from a wad of newspaper taped all around. See how far he can make it go. Kick it and chase it!

Notes:

Don't Forget! Activities should be supervised at all times by an adult. Any material, food, or toy given to a young child should be reviewed for safety.

 ASQ3

Fine Motor

Activities to Help Your Toddler Grow and Learn

Your toddler is becoming more skilled with hands and fingers. She can play with and use toys in many ways, including stacking, poking, pushing, and pulling. She is also gaining skill at holding and using crayons or washable markers. She knows to take apart pieces of a simple puzzle and may try to put the pieces back together.

Tear It Up	After you each wash your hands, show your child how to tear lettuce or spinach leaves into a bowl. Help her tear small pieces just right to eat. Be sure to tell the family who made the salad. Your child also may like tearing strips of magazines or junk mail.
Aim and Drop	Show your little one how to drop a clothespin, spool, or dry pasta (uncooked) into an empty milk jug or plastic container with a large opening. Play the game as long as your toddler enjoys it. Let him shake the container and enjoy the sound.
Stacking Blocks	Let your little one play with small wooden cubes or blocks. Little plastic containers can be washed out and stacked, too. Show her how to stack one on top of another. Build a tower. Count aloud as you stack the blocks so that she begins to hear the sound of numbers. She'll love knocking down the tower.
String a Snack	Give your toddler a small container of round cereal pieces and a piece of string with tape around the end to make it stiff. Show him how to string the cereal. He can wear his necklace or nibble on it!
Place Mats	Make sure your toddler gets lots of chances to practice writing and drawing. You might keep paper and crayons or washable markers in the kitchen so you can keep an eye on her while getting dinner ready. Use drawings for placemats for the family. She will be so proud!
Help Make a Snack	Let your toddler help make a snack. He can unscrew lids from containers such as applesauce once you get the lid loosened. He can help scoop and/or spread butter with a plastic knife. He can also help eat. Yummy!

Notes:

Don't Forget! Activities should be supervised at all times by an adult. Any material, food, or toy given to a young child should be reviewed for safety.

Problem Solving

Activities to Help Your Toddler Grow and Learn

Your busy learner now recognizes pictures of animals and other pictures, such as pictures of family members. He enjoys a lot of new activities with your help, such as painting and playing with playdough. He is beginning to understand about things that are similar or that go together in some way. He is very curious about how things work.

Copy Cat	On a large piece of paper, draw and scribble together with your toddler. Take turns. You scribble, and then let her scribble. You draw a line, and then let her draw a line. Let her take a turn, and then you copy her scribbles.
Making Things Fit	Allow your child to play with puzzles or toys that fit together or inside each other. Plastic containers that nest are also fun. Use the word *fit* when you can: "That piece *fits* in the puzzle."
Tool Play	Help your child play games or do tasks that use tools. For example, use a sponge to wipe off a chair. Use a strainer and a scoop to play in the sand. Use measuring cups and funnels to fill up containers in the bathtub. Be sure to use the correct names for these items. You'll be surprised at how fast your busy little one learns them.
Match the Socks	When you fold laundry, set aside some of the socks, both large and small. Show your toddler one sock of a pair and let him find the other. Show him how to match the socks if he needs help. Ask him, "Whose big blue socks are these?" and "Where is the other one like this?"
Nature Walk	Go on a neighborhood walk, collecting little things such as rocks and leaves in a small pail or plastic tub. At home, try to put things together into different groups. For example, help your child sort big and little rocks, rocks from leaves, or black rocks from white rocks. Your child will learn about grouping things.
Matching Pictures	Cut out pictures of toys, food, and other familiar objects, and glue them on cards. Have your child try to match cards to actual objects in your home. Show your child a picture of a toothbrush. Ask him, "Where is a toothbrush like this?" Then show him a picture of a chair: "Can you find something like this?"

Notes:

Don't Forget! Activities should be supervised at all times by an adult. Any material, food, or toy given to a young child should be reviewed for safety. Make sure your toddler doesn't put anything in her mouth while playing outside.

ASQ-3™ Learning Activities by Elizabeth Twombly and Ginger Fink.
Copyright © 2013 by Paul H. Brookes Publishing Co. All rights reserved.

57

Personal-Social
Activities to Help Your Toddler Grow and Learn

16–20 months

Your toddler is gaining more independence every day. She may show jealousy if others get attention, especially siblings. She is very interested in other children. She likes to do things by herself and may become a little bossy and resist your suggestions. Your good humor will go far in seeing you both through the coming months.

Big Time Mealtime	When the family is at the table for meals, encourage your toddler to eat with his own utensils. He may need a booster seat to reach the table. He can begin to drink from a small plastic cup (just don't fill it to the top). Talk about what a big boy he is.
Family Dancing	Show your toddler how to dance. Play music, and show her how to follow you or dance with you. Invite other family members to dance along. Pick up your toddler and dance with her. Praise your little one. Give her a hug.
Storytime	This is a good time to make a routine of reading stories every night before bed. After getting ready for bed, cuddle up to enjoy a favorite book. It is especially good to read with the television turned off. Your child will hear the words and the expression in your voice. This also might be a special time for another member of the family to read with your toddler.
Comfort Me	Your toddler is busy and often frustrated. He will need a lot of comfort and support to understand his feelings. He responds to what he's feeling right now and does not know that he will feel better in a little while. Give him words for how he is feeling: "You are sad that mom is leaving. I will be back after nap" or "It's really frustrating when you can't get that sock on." He will need your warm voice, a hug, and comfort.
Helping Hands	Your child can begin to help in little ways. She can use a sponge to wipe up the table after dinner. She can put toys or socks in a basket. She will feel good about helping. Let her know you notice: "What a big helper!"
Tickles and Kisses	While getting your toddler ready for bed, say goodnight with a little tickle or kiss to different parts of baby: "Goodnight, little nose [tickle]. Goodnight, little foot [tickle]. Goodnight, little ear [tickle]." Ask him what part needs a goodnight tickle or a goodnight kiss.
Bear Bedtime	Let your child put a doll or stuffed animal to bed. She can help her bear brush his teeth. Read bear a story. Tuck bear in and kiss him goodnight.

Notes:

Don't Forget! Activities should be supervised at all times by an adult. Any material, food, or toy given to a young child should be reviewed for safety. Always watch your toddler during mealtime.

Communication

Activities to Help Your Toddler Grow and Learn

Your toddler is learning language very quickly and will imitate words he hears, good or bad. He is using different types of words and putting them together in short phrases. Most of his words are understandable. He may be starting to sing simple songs. He may also be testing the power of words by using the strong words "no" and "mine."

Sock Puppet	Put your hand in a clean sock and make it talk: "Hi, my name is José. I am visiting you. What is your name?" Your child might say something or want to touch the puppet. Keep the conversation going. Let the puppet give your toddler a kiss!
Construction Time	Collect materials to make a pretend airport, street, or neighborhood. Masking tape can be the runway or the road. Oatmeal containers can be tunnels. Cereal boxes can be buildings. Cardboard can make a ramp for cars to go *up* and *down*. Toy cars can go *through* the tunnel, *under* the bridge, or *beside* a building. Use these new words while your child builds and plays.
Fun with Books	Find large picture books and/or magazines to look at with your child. Point to pictures and talk about what you see. Ask her, "Where's the doggie?" and have her point to a picture. Let your child "read" to someone else, such as Grandpa. If your child is beginning to learn about using the toilet, this is a good time to put a small basket of picture books in the bathroom to "read."
Field Trips	Your toddler will enjoy going to new places, even to a new store. This is a great time to learn new words. Talk to him about what you are seeing: "Look, that fruit is called a *mango*. Look at that big refrigerator. Put your hand on the door—it's very *cold*."
Sing Together	Your child will love learning simple songs such as "Twinkle, Twinkle, Little Star." Teach your child simple songs you remember from childhood. Enjoy singing together. Later, ask your child to sing for someone else in the family.
Car Talk	Teach your child words about the car as you get in or out during the day. Talk about what you're doing: "Let's *open* the car door and get inside. I'm going to *buckle* your car seat. Daddy's going to *close and lock* the door. See the *lights* go out? Do you hear the *motor*? Let's go!" Soon your little rider will know all about the car.

Notes:

Don't Forget! Activities should be supervised at all times by an adult. Any material, food or toy given, to a young child should be reviewed for safety.

Gross Motor

Activities to Help Your Toddler Grow and Learn

Your toddler is busy and fast! She is running and learning to kick and jump. Her leg muscles are getting stronger, and she can walk up and down stairs holding on to your hand or a railing. She really enjoys moving her body and learning new skills. She also likes to climb, so be watchful!

Froggie Jump	Hold your child's hands and help him jump off a low step. Then let him try it by himself. Once he can do this, show your child how to jump over something, such as a small milk carton. Encourage your child: "Wow! You can jump just like a frog."
Bowling Adventure	Show your child how to roll a medium-size ball toward pins to knock them down. Balls can be made from wads of newspaper taped all around. Empty milk cartons or plastic soda bottles can be used for pins. When your child gets tired of bowling, you can play kickball.
Balancing Practice	Assist your child by holding her hand, then ask her to stand on one foot. Now ask her to stand on the other foot. See if she can stand without holding your hand. Count how many seconds she can balance. Keep practicing!
Let's Go for a Ride	Give your child a riding toy without pedals. It will help him control the movement of the toy and strengthen his legs. Later he will enjoy riding a tricycle with pedals.
Dance to the Music	Play different kinds of music that you and your child enjoy: salsa, hip-hop, country, classical, jazz. Dance and move to the music with your child. Sometimes pick her up so she can feel you move. Mostly, let her dance and move by herself. She may enjoy dancing with scarves or ribbons. Shakers and bells make it great fun!
Trip to the Playground	Find a playground in your neighborhood and have some fun! Run, swing, and climb. As you walk to the playground, practice stepping up or down street curbs or stones holding your child's hand. If there are stairs or ladders, encourage him to walk or climb up. Hold on to the railing!
Red Light, Green Light	When you are in a safe open space, teach your child this game. Hold her hand and say, "Green light," to begin the run. Say, "Red light," to stop quickly, then "Green light" again. When she knows the game, she can run toward you by herself while you say, "Green light! Red light!" Your open arms are the finish line.

Notes:

Don't Forget! Activities should be supervised at all times by an adult. Any material, food, or toy given to a young child should be reviewed for safety.

Fine Motor
Activities to Help Your Toddler Grow and Learn

Your busy toddler enjoys activities that build small muscles. He can stack and build with small toys. He is learning how to hold a crayon with his thumb and fingers and how to scribble circles and lines. He is becoming more skilled at stringing beads and doing other activities using two hands.

Stack It Up

Your child will have fun stacking small things and knocking them down. Use blocks, paper or plastic cups, small boxes, or anything stackable. Count how many things your child can stack. See how high she can go!

String Fling

String beads, macaroni, or large cereal. Help your child practice using two hands at one time. A shoelace or string with some tape on the end will work well for stringing. Make a necklace for someone special!

My Family Book

Make a small picture album for your toddler. Include pictures of family members, friends, and pets. Look through the album and talk about each person. Have him turn pages and tell you about the pictures. Have him share his special book with visitors.

Beginning Puzzles

Show your toddler how to put beginning puzzles together. You can make a puzzle by cutting the front of a cereal box into two or three wide strips. Help her aim and place the piece in the right place if she needs help. Praise her for trying: "Good for you! You can do it!"

Letters and Shopping Lists

When you make your shopping list or write a letter, have paper and a pen or crayon for your child to write along with you. Say, "I'm writing a letter to Grandma. You can write one, too." Send the letters in the mail. Grandma may write back!

Make Fruit Salad

Let your child use a Popsicle stick or a plastic picnic knife to help you cut bits of fruit, such as banana or peaches. He can help scoop yogurt, sprinkle in raisins, and stir everything together. Don't forget to tell the family who made the salad.

Snack-Time Helper

Your child will enjoy making her own snack. She can help twist open lids on jars; open containers; spread cream cheese, hummus, butter, jam, or jelly; scoop out applesauce; and more. The more she can do herself (with your support), the faster she will learn and the more skilled she will become.

Notes:

Don't Forget! Activities should be supervised at all times by an adult. Any material, food, or toy given to a young child should be reviewed for safety. Always watch your toddler during mealtimes.

Problem Solving

Activities to Help Your Toddler Grow and Learn

Your toddler is curious about body parts and what they do. She understands more about how things go together, such as where items belong. She knows that a picture of a cat stands for a real cat, and she is learning what objects are used for. Her busy mind is trying to make sense of what she sees and experiences.

Scoop and Pour	Let your child practice pouring and filling. Provide recycled materials, such as clean milk cartons, yogurt cups, detergent scoops, and plastic bottles for playing in the sand or water. She could play with these in the tub. Put uncooked rice or popcorn in a large tray or box with scoops and containers. Talk about what your child is doing, and use new words such as *empty, full, pouring,* and *scooping.*
Household Helper	For pretend play, make a box with household tools, such as paintbrushes, a small shovel, a small broom, or a dry sponge. Your child can pretend to wipe the table, paint a wall, dig in the garden, or sweep the floor. Talk about all the work getting done: "Wow, that floor is looking good."
I Can Do, Can You?	During bath time or lap time with your child, play a follow-the-leader game. Say, "My eyes blink. Show me how your eyes blink. My nose can sniff. Can your nose sniff? I can clap my hands. Can you clap, too?" Do something silly!
The Doctor Is In	Tell your toddler a doll or stuffed animal is sick. Make a doctor's office by folding a sheet on the floor or on a low table for the examination. Make bandages with tape and tissue. If the doll's arm is hurt, you can make a sling made out of a napkin or handkerchief. The doll will need lots of comfort, so encourage lots of hugs.
Topsy Turvy	Turn a cup or a box of cereal upside down during breakfast. See if your child notices and turns it back the right way. Try this at other times of the day. For example, hold the book upside down when reading to your child and see what happens. Have fun with this silly game.
Train Tracks	While your child is watching, draw two long horizontal lines about 4 inches apart on a large sheet of paper. Then, show your child how to draw vertical lines from one to the other. Encourage him to make a lot of these vertical lines. The design will look like a train track. Bring out the trains or cars to play on the train track.

Notes:

Don't Forget! Activities should be supervised at all times by an adult. Any material, food, or toy given to a young child should be reviewed for safety. Always watch your toddler during bath time.

Personal-Social
Activities to Help Your Toddler Grow and Learn

Your toddler is becoming very independent. He will want to do everything by himself, even if he isn't quite able. He wants things *now* and quickly becomes frustrated if that doesn't happen. He enjoys playing close to other children but is not really able to share just yet. He likes to initiate simple household tasks and can put some of his toys away with help from you.

Baby Bear Beds	Make a bed for your child's doll or a stuffed animal using a shoebox. A small piece of cloth or a dishtowel makes a blanket or a pillow. Your child can help her baby go to bed at night. She can read a story and tuck him into his new bed. Don't forget a kiss!
Play Dates	Your child needs your help playing with others but enjoys being with other children. Stay close by when he is with other children. Have a lot of the same kinds of toys to help the children cooperate. Several trucks, cars, and dolls are easier to share than one of each kind. Let him know when he plays well with another child: "You gave the car to Jamie—you *shared*."
Dress-Up Time	Make a bag or box with simple dress-up clothing, such as hats, shoes, a purse, and other special clothes that are easy to wear. Your child may need some help but will have a lot of fun pretending. Don't forget to let her look in the mirror: "Look at that big girl all dressed up. Is that Mia?"
Playing House	Make simple playhouse furniture for your child. Turn a box over and draw burners to make a stove. Place a plastic tub or dishpan on another low box or table for "washing dishes." Add a doll, stuffed animal, plastic plates, cups, a dish towel, and some safe cooking utensils. Your child can "cook" at his stove while you cook dinner. Follow your child's lead. Talk and have fun!
Picnic Outing	Find a place to have a picnic with your child. The park or playground is fun, but your child will have fun even if the picnic is inside your home. Let your child help prepare some simple food and drinks for the picnic. Maybe the stuffed animals would like to join you. Let your child practice feeding herself.
Washing Hands	Help your child learn all of the steps in washing hands. You can do this before or after meals, before bedtime, and after going potty. Stay close by while he learns to stand on a stool, turn on the water, wash hands with soap, and rinse and dry hands with a towel. Singing a song makes it fun: "This is the way we wash our hands, wash our hands, wash our hands. This is the way we wash our hands, before we eat our food."

Notes:

Don't Forget! Activities should be supervised at all times by an adult. Any material, food, or toy given to a young child should be reviewed for safety. Always watch your toddler during mealtime.

Communication

Activities to Help Your Toddler Grow and Learn

Your toddler enjoys being with you and is learning new words very quickly. She is using her language more often to let you know her wants, needs, and ideas. She can carry on a simple conversation and may talk to herself or pretend to have a conversation with a stuffed animal. She can follow simple directions and loves to read books. She likes to hear the same book read over and over!

I Spy	You can play this in the car, on the bus, or on a walk. Say, "I spy with my little eye a green truck." Your child tries to find what you spied. Then it is his turn to spy something. Remember to spy things your child can see. You can also say, "I hear with my little ear…" Listen for sounds such as a motorcycle, a car horn, a bird singing, a dog barking, or a radio.
Picture Album	Make a little album with pictures of your child and the people and pets he knows. Have your child talk about the pictures and name the people and pets. Ask your child, "Who's that? What are they doing?" Look at this book over and over. Help your child learn to say her first and last name and write it on the album.
When You Were Little	Tell your child stories about when he was little: "When you were first born…" or "When you were a little baby…" Your child will love to hear these stories again and again.
Dinner Report	At the end of a busy day, let everyone talk about his or her day. Ask your child to tell the family what she did during the day. Let her take her time. You might remind her if she forgets some events. Soon she will learn to tell what happened in the right order. Say, "Thanks for telling us about your day!"
Washing a Baby	Let your child wash a baby doll in a plastic tub, or bring a baby doll into his bath. Name the doll's body parts as he washes the baby: "You're washing the baby's hands." Let your child know what a good job he is doing taking care of the baby.
What's that Sound?	Turn off the television and other electronics, and listen with your child to sounds around your home. Listen to the refrigerator motor, wind chimes, a clock ticking, or people talking. Ask your child to tell you what she hears. Try this at night. Listen for the night sounds of crickets, frogs, or cars beeping. Whisper to each other about what you hear.

Notes:

 Don't Forget! Activities should be supervised at all times by an adult. Any material, food, or toy given to a young child should be reviewed for safety.

Gross Motor

Activities to Help Your Toddler Grow and Learn

The word *active* still best describes your toddler. His muscles are getting stronger. He is more confident with his abilities. Let your toddler continue physical activities he enjoys, such as kicking balls, riding toys, climbing jungle gyms, swinging, running, jumping, and balancing.

Can You Do This?	Stand on one foot. Ask your child, "Can you do this?" Even if your child stands only for 1 second, praise her. Pretend to be an airplane flying with your arms out across the room. Jump, crawl, gallop, and tiptoe around the house. Let your child be the leader and copy her. Play with the whole family.
Jumping Frog Contest	Pretend you and your child are frogs or rabbits, and show your child how to jump with both feet together. Then jump over a chalk line, crack in the sidewalk, or small object. Make marks with chalk to measure how far he can jump with both feet together: "Wow, look how far the frog jumped that time!"
Soccer Star	Use a medium-size ball (8–10 inches) to play soccer with your child. Set up a goal with two empty milk cartons or turn a large cardboard box on its side. Encourage your child to kick the ball through the cartons or into the box. Great goal!
Playground Fun	Just about every day is a good day to spend time outside in the yard or on a playground. Encourage your child to run, swing, and climb up play structures and slide down slides. Join your child in these activities. Jump over cracks or sticks on the way to the playground. Help your child practice stepping up and down stairs or jumping down from short steps. Meet other children and parents. Have a great time!
Basketball Hoops	Stand in front of your child and hold out your arms in a circle. You are the "hoop." Encourage your child to toss a soft ball into your "basket." You can also use a clean garbage can or laundry basket for a target. Celebrate when your child makes a basket!
Horsing Around	Bounce your toddler on your knees or hold his hands and let him straddle and ride your foot. If you cross your legs, it is less tiring to bounce him. Stop bouncing and wait for him to bounce or ask for more. Ask your child, "More? Do you want to ride some more?"
Stair-Stepping Solo	When you climb stairs, let your toddler hold on to only one of your fingers. You may have to slow down, but let her climb the stairs with little support or all by herself. Show her the stair rail and encourage her to hold it for support. When your child climbs all by herself, give her a big hug!

Notes:

Don't Forget! Activities should be supervised at all times by an adult. Any material, food, or toy given to a young child should be reviewed for safety.

Fine Motor

Activities to Help Your Toddler Grow and Learn

24–30 months

Your toddler's eyes and hands are working together well. He enjoys taking apart and putting together small things. He loves using any kind of writing or drawing tool. Provide scrap paper, washable crayons, or markers. You can also try puzzles, blocks, and other safe small toys. Talk and enjoy the time together. When writing or drawing, set up clear rules: "We draw *only on the paper, and only on the table.* I will help you remember."

Flipping Pancakes	Trim the corners from a simple sponge to form a "pancake." Give your child a small frying pan and a spatula. Show him how to flip the pancake.
Macaroni String	String a necklace out of dried pasta with big holes. Tube-shaped pasta, such as rigatoni, works really well. Your child can paint the pasta before or after stringing it. Make sure she has a string with a stiff tip, such as a shoelace. You can also tape the ends of a piece of yarn so that it is easy to string.
Homemade Orange Juice	Make orange juice or lemonade with your toddler. Have him help squeeze the fruit using a handheld juicer. Show him how to twist the fruit back and forth to get the juice out. To make lemonade, you will need to add some sugar and water. Let him help you stir it all up. Cheers!
Draw What I Draw	Have your child copy a line that you draw, up and down and side to side. You take a turn. Then your child takes a turn. Try zigzag patterns and spirals. Use a crayon and paper, a stick in the sand, markers on newspaper, or your fingers on a steamy bathroom mirror.
Bath-Time Fun	At bath time, let your toddler play with things to squeeze, such as a sponge, a washcloth, or a squeeze toy. Squeezing really helps strengthen the muscles in her hands and fingers. Plus it makes bath time more fun!
My Favorite Things	Your child can make a book about all of his favorite things. Clip or staple a few pieces of paper together for him. He can choose his favorite color. Let him show you what pictures to cut from magazines. He may even try cutting all by himself. Glue pictures on the pages. Your child can use markers or crayons to decorate pages. Stickers can be fun, too. You can write down what he says about each page. Let him "write" his own name. It may only be a mark, but that's a start!
Sorting Objects	Find an egg carton or muffin pan. Put some common objects such as nuts, shells, or cotton balls into a plastic bowl. Let your toddler use a little spoon or tongs to pick up the objects and put them in different sections of the egg carton. Give her a little hug when she has success!

Notes:

Don't Forget! Activities should be supervised at all times by an adult. Any material, food, or toy given to a young child should be reviewed for safety. Always watch your toddler during mealtime and bath time. Make sure she doesn't put the sorting objects in her mouth.

 ASQ-3

Problem Solving
Activities to Help Your Toddler Grow and Learn

Doing things all by herself is very important for your toddler. Be patient and enjoy this time of growing independence, even though it may sometimes be frustrating. Give your child plenty of time and chances to figure out and do things by herself. Although make-believe is an important part of your toddler's growth, real and make-believe can be confusing. Help your child learn the difference especially if she sees something on television or in a movie.

Paper Bag Matching Game	Gather two of several household objects. Use two paper bags with the same things in each bag. Pull one item out and ask your child to reach in and find one in his bag. Remind your child, "No peeking, just feeling!"
Helping Around the House	Ask your toddler to help with the laundry. Sort by color or put similar things in one place. Let your child help you put all of the socks in one pile and all of the shirts in another. She can line up shoes and boots in the right place, and you can help her make sure they are in pairs.
Snack-Time Roundup	Give your child a snack with many pieces, such as cut-up fruit, small crackers, or cereal loops. Make a line of four things and count them as you put them in front of him. Give him four pieces and see if he can make a line, too. You can help your toddler count the food pieces and then eat them up.
Building with Boxes	Gather up several small- and medium-size boxes to use as building blocks. You can use shoe boxes, cereal boxes, clean milk cartons, and so forth. Encourage your child to build with the boxes. Make comments or ask questions: "You are making that so tall. Is that a house? Is it a wall?" Add toy cars or animals for more fun.
Where Is It?	Using any object in your house, play a hiding game with your toddler. For example, hide a teddy bear under a pillow. Give your toddler clues to find the bear: "Where's bear? Can you find her? She's under something green" or "She is behind something soft." Give your toddler help as needed. Then let him hide things and give you some clues.
Bring Me Something	Make a game of asking your child to bring you certain types of objects. Teach her about texture by asking her to bring soft or hard things. Help your child learn colors by asking for items of a certain shade. Talk about what she brings you: "Is your toy train hard or soft?"

Notes:

 Don't Forget! Activities should be supervised at all times by an adult. Any material, food, or toy given to a young child should be reviewed for safety. Always watch your toddler during mealtime.

Personal-Social

Activities to Help Your Toddler Grow and Learn

24–30 months

Your toddler is still learning to do things for himself and wants very much to please adults. He enjoys feeding and dressing himself without your help. Toddlers love to imitate, so you can let him help around the house with simple tasks, such as wiping spills. Your extra support and patience will make life easier for both of you, especially if there's a new baby at home.

Dapper Dresser	Taking off clothing is easy! Now have your toddler put on her own clothes. Start with loose shorts. Have her sit on the floor, put both legs in the shorts, stand up, and pull up the shorts. Tell your child, "Wow! You put those on all by yourself!" Let her look at herself in a mirror. Practice putting on a T-shirt, with her head first ("Boo!"), then one arm, and then the other arm. Say, "What an excellent dresser you are!"
Playmates	Invite your child's friend over to play for a short time, or take your child to a relative's or friend's house where there is someone his age. Make sure there are enough toys to share easily. Later, let him tell you all about his play date.
First Feelings	Help your child name feelings when they happen. You can help her understand feeling *worried* by telling her, "You look worried. Can you tell me about it?" If you know your child is frustrated, use the words: "I know you are really *frustrated*, but you can have a turn in a minute." When your child learns that feelings have names, she will be able to handle them more easily.
Holding a Baby	Let your child hold a baby sibling or cousin. Help your child as he holds the baby so that he can sit steadily and use his arms to support the baby. Talk about how babies must be handled gently. Tell him what a good friend he is to the baby and how baby likes him.
All by Myself	During a meal, let your little one feed herself using a fork, spoon, or other utensil. Mashed potatoes will be a little easier than peas, but soon she will master peas, too! Show her how to twist noodles with a fork. Have an extra napkin and sponge on hand!
Big Little Parent	When your toddler plays with a doll or stuffed animal, give him a small plastic dish, a spoon, and a cup. He may also need a baby blanket and maybe a hairbrush and toothbrush. Now he can really take care of that baby bear!

Notes:

Don't Forget! Activities should be supervised at all times by an adult. Any material, food, or toy given to a young child should be reviewed for safety. Always watch your toddler during mealtime.

ASQ·3

Communication

Activities to Help Your Child Grow and Learn

Your child can talk about many things and can follow simple directions. She will make mistakes with her grammar, such as saying "foots" instead of *feet*. Your child can tell you what's happening. She is using longer sentences now. Talk about what happened during the day. Read to your child every day. She might even pretend to read favorite books by herself, using the words you have read to her.

Reading Magazines	Talk about the pictures in magazines. Find pictures that your child will recognize, such as toothpaste, soap, diapers, pets, or cars. Point to the picture and ask, "What is this? Do we have this at home? What do we do with this?"
Silly Me	Your child will have fun when you act silly. Pretend you don't know what things really are. Point to the toothpaste and ask your child, "Is that the soap?" Let him tell you what it really is. Act surprised. Your child will enjoy "teaching" you the right name of things.
Bandage Game	Make pretend bandages using tape or stickers. Ask your child, "Where is your cut?" See how many body parts your child can name. Give her some help for the tricky ones, "Oh, you hurt your wrist." Put a bandage on each part. You can wash the bandage off during bath time. This game can also be played with a doll or stuffed animal.
Let's Put Things Away	Have your child help you put away things like food or folded laundry. Use words such as *up, down, over,* or *through:* "Please put the can *on* the shelf" or "Please put your socks *in* the drawer." Thanks for the help! You can give silly directions, too: "Put the lemons *under* the chair."
What's Going On?	Ask your child to tell you what is happening in a picture in a book or magazine: "What is the baby doing? What is the dog doing?" Then, listen carefully to your child's interesting story.
What's Your Name?	Play this silly name game. When you greet your child, act as if you don't know who he is. Say, "Hello, little boy. What's your name?" When he tells you, greet him with happy surprise: "Oh, you're my little boy! I'm so happy to see you!"

Notes:

Don't Forget! Activities should be supervised at all times by an adult. Any material, food, or toy given to a young child should be reviewed for safety.

Gross Motor

Activities to Help Your Child Grow and Learn

Your child is improving skills using his leg and arm muscles. He is working on making these muscles stronger, more flexible, and more coordinated. He can catch an 8-inch ball, jump about 2 feet, make sharp turns around a corner while running, and avoid obstacles in his path.

Over the River	When playing outside, place a towel or piece of cloth about 2 feet wide on the grass. This is the "river." Have your child run and jump over the river without "getting wet." At first, you can fold the towel so that the river is not so wide. Then, you can make it bigger. Watch out for alligators!
Balloon Kick	Let your child kick a balloon from one end of the room to the other. Lay a box on its side for a goal. See if she can kick the balloon into the box.
Animal Walk	Show your child how to move like different animals. Can he waddle like a duck or walk on all fours like a dog? Encourage him to pretend to be these animals and make noises like them. Play along. Call the cat: "Here, kitty, kitty." Balance on one foot like a pink flamingo.
Heel-to-Toe Walk	Show your child how to walk heel to toe along a line on the sidewalk or a short length of clothesline on the ground. She can stretch her arms to keep her balance. She can hold an umbrella and pretend she is walking a tightrope in a circus!
Basketball	Place an empty laundry basket on the floor against a wall. Give your child a soft ball about 4 inches in size. Place a string or piece of tape on the floor for a throw line. Show your child how to throw overhand to get the ball in the basket. Start about 4 feet back from the basket. Move back as your child gets better.
Chasing Bubbles	Go outside on a nice day to blow bubbles. Ask your child to clap his hands together and pop them. Blow some bubbles high so that your child needs to jump to pop them. Blow some far away so that your child will need to run to pop them. Clap big ones and then clap little ones. When you're done, go wash those soapy hands!

Notes:

Don't Forget! Activities should be supervised at all times by an adult. Any material, food, or toy given to a young child should be reviewed for safety.

Fine Motor

Activities to Help Your Child Grow and Learn

30–36 months

Your child is learning to hold pens, crayons, and markers with her thumb and two fingers just like adults do. She has learned to make scissors open and close and can make snips in paper when you hold it. She can use her two hands together with small toys, such as interlocking blocks or stringing beads. She can put together puzzles with five or more pieces.

Yummy Puzzles	Cut off the front part of a cereal box. Now cut this into four or five puzzle pieces. Your child will have fun putting this simple puzzle together. He may need a little help at first.
Little Writer	Show your child how to make lines and circles or even simple shapes. Circles and straight lines will be easiest for your child to copy. Your child may want to learn to write the first letter of her name. Keep it fun! It is okay if your child's marks don't look much like real letters. Encourage her attempts: "You're a good writer!"
Tong Time	Give your child a pair of small kitchen tongs, children's chopsticks, or tweezers. See if he can move cotton balls or dry macaroni from one container into another. Then try something heavier such as walnuts, spools, or small stones.
Junior Mechanic	Collect large bolts, matching nuts, and even washers. Your child will enjoy matching the bolt to the nut and twisting them together.
Little Flicker	Make little balls of newspaper about the size of marbles and show your child how to "flick" a ball across a tabletop or space on the floor into an open box or at a target. Use thumb and index finger to "flick." See how far your child can flick the paper balls or hit the target. This game can bring lots of laughs!
Bubbles!	Let your child use washable crayons or markers to draw bubbles on paper. Let him draw as many as he wants and color them in. Show him how to draw big bubbles and little bubbles, purple bubbles and green bubbles. Now that he has drawn so many bubbles, maybe it's time to blow some real bubbles!

Notes:

Don't Forget! Activities should be supervised at all times by an adult. Any material, food, or toy given to a young child should be reviewed for safety. Make sure your child does not put any objects in her mouth.

Problem Solving
Activities to Help Your Child Grow and Learn

Your child can notice how things are the same and how they are different. He knows about colors, long and short, a little and a lot, and which one of your kitchen spoons is the biggest. With your help, he can put three things of different sizes in order from small to large. Pretend play is still very important and fun for both of you!

What Is This?	After giving your child a bath, stand or seat your child in front of a mirror. With a towel, dry different parts of her body. While drying her hair, be silly and ask, "What is this stuff?" While drying her shoulder, ask, "What is this thing?" While drying ribs, ask, "What are these bony things?" Have fun being together while tickling, cuddling, and teaching the names of body parts.
Making Trains	Line up four to five small cars or other objects in a row to make a "train." Make sure your child sees what you did. Now give your child some objects to line up and make a train. You can line up different things, such as blocks, spoons, or shells. Say, "Wow, look at your train. Where is it going?"
Big and Little	Show your child two items of different sizes, such as shoes, cups, or spoons. Talk about the big one and the little one. Talk about the size of things in your house, at the park, or at the supermarket: "Wow. Look at that pumpkin. It's really big!" Add a medium-size item and try playing Big, Little, and One in the Middle.
Tell Me Your Story	Give your child plain paper and a few washable crayons or markers for drawing. Ask her to tell you about what she drew. Write the story on your child's paper. Print her name. Tell her, "This is your story, and this is your name." Read the story to someone important.
Reading the Neighborhood	Show your child signs in your neighborhood, such as a stop sign. Tell him what it means. Point out the railroad sign and tell him it's where the trains go. In a restaurant, show your child the different pictures on rest room doors, one for girls and one for boys. Look at the painted crosswalk on the street. Next time you go out, ask him to read signs with you.
Silly Sounds	Play a silly copy game with your child in the car or on the bus. For example, tell her a silly phrase like, "Bee, zim, zop." See if your child can copy you. Let your child make up a silly phrase and copy her. Now make up a silly song to sing!

Notes:

Personal-Social

Activities to Help Your Child Grow and Learn

30–36 months

Your child is able to take care of some of her personal needs, but she still needs your hugs and support. With a little help, she can usually separate from you in familiar settings. She can obey simple rules. She enjoys simple games with other children and is proud of her accomplishments. She will respond with pride when you notice positive behavior, such as being helpful, following a rule, or doing something for herself.

Cooking Helper	Let your child help with cooking by measuring, pouring, stirring, washing, and tearing greens. With your help and a plastic knife, he can even cut soft foods, such as bananas. These are real activities that help the family. Tell him, "Thank you for helping with our meal!" Ask him to tell the family what is in the salad. Yum!
Super Picker-Upper	Show your child how to put trash in the trash can. If your child drops paper, ask her to pick it up and put it into the trash can. She may enjoy helping you put trash outside for the garbage truck to pick up. Show your child how important it is to keep the world clean. Talk about what would happen if people didn't pick up trash.
Bathing Beauty	Your child will enjoy trying to wash himself in the bathtub. Show him how to use a washcloth and soap. Be sure to let your child know that he is doing a good job. Then, give your child a towel to dry himself: "Whose clean little boy is this?" Have fun!
Naming Feelings	Help your child understand feelings by noticing them and naming them. Children need to learn that other people have feelings, too: "When you take the toy, it makes your sister sad." Don't be afraid to use big words: "I can tell you're *excited* because it's your birthday!"
Super Driver	Make an obstacle course in your home or outside. Let your little driver push a cart or pull a wagon, steering around boxes, rocks, or over a hose. There's a big hug at the finish line!
Look at You!	Start a dress-up bin for your child. Go through your closet and gather old clothes. Gather men's items as well. Old purses, wallets, hats, ties, shoes, belts, and necklaces are fun. Let your child dress up and look in the mirror. Be prepared to play for a while. Have your camera ready!

Notes:

Don't Forget! Activities should be supervised at all times by an adult. Any material, food, or toy given to a young child should be reviewed for safety. Always watch your child during mealtime and bath time.

Communication

Activities to Help Your Child Grow and Learn

Your child is learning to use complete sentences to tell you all about what's happening. He also can follow more than one direction at a time. He has probably learned both his first and last name and can tell you if you ask. He loves to have conversations with a friend or maybe a toy doll or bear. He has learned that a voice on the telephone really comes from a person, even though he can't see the speaker, and your child is more likely to talk than just listen.

Good Night	When it's time to go to bed, give goodnight kisses all over. Tell your child, "I'm going to kiss you on your knee. I'm going to kiss you on top of your head. Now I'm going to kiss you behind your ear. Good night back there! Good night everywhere!"
Who's This Person?	Pretend you suddenly forgot who your child is. Say, "What's your name, little girl? Is it Samantha? Is it Rosita? Do you have another name?" When she tells you her name, you can be very happily surprised!
Love Notes	Put little notes to your child here and there. A note might say, "You are a very helpful brother to your baby sister." A note on your child's toy shelf can say you noticed that the toys were put away. A note by the plate at dinnertime can say that Dad will read a favorite story at bedtime. Read these notes to your little one so that he learns reading is fun and important.
Where the Creatures Live	Go for a walk outside and look for living things. Ask your child questions about the world around her. "Where do we see birds?" Up in the sky. "Where do bugs live?" Under rocks. Your child may need a little help at first, but soon she will know the answers.
Weather Person	At the start of the day, ask your child to look out the window and tell you about the weather. Is it sunny? Is it raining? Is it cloudy? What will the weather be today? Have your child draw a picture of the sun if the day is sunny, raindrops if the day is rainy, and clouds if the sky is cloudy.
A Card of Love	Collect paper and glue; little craft items such as stickers, stamps, or ribbons; and pictures of favorite things and animals. Make a birthday or greeting card for someone special. Talk about this person, and help your child write a message. Address the card, stamp it, and mail it. This little kindness will bring much appreciation.

Notes:

Don't Forget! Activities should be supervised at all times by an adult. Any material, food, or toy given to a young child should be reviewed for safety.

ASQ-3™ Learning Activities by Elizabeth Twombly and Ginger Fink.

91

Gross Motor

Activities to Help Your Child Grow and Learn

Your child can usually kick a ball forward, jump, and perhaps hop on one foot. She likes to do things for longer periods of time now and may spend quite a long time riding a tricycle or pulling things in a wagon. Climbing is getting to be one of her favorite activities. She also enjoys active play with friends. Having used all that energy, she will usually sleep well through the night.

Marching in the Band	Show your active child how to march like a member of the band. Be sure to get those knees up high! Invite a friend to join you. Add a drum and a flag and make a parade!
Kangaroo Kid	Show your child how a kangaroo jumps around. Pretend to be a mother kangaroo. With your feet together, jump, jump, jump. Call for your baby kangaroo to follow you. This is fun outdoors or with a friend.
Freeze!	Let your child dance or move around in any way he wants. When you say, "Freeze," he has to stop right away in the middle of a motion. Start the movement up again by saying, "Melt." Take turns playing this silly game.
Soccer Fun	Give your child a medium-size ball. Show her how to kick it by swinging a foot back, then forward. Turn a cardboard box on its side and encourage your child to kick the ball into the box for a goal. Shout, "Goal!" when your child gets the ball into the box.
Airplanes Everywhere	Let your child pretend to be an airplane and run with arms outstretched. Show him how to lean to the left, then to the right. Make some airplane noises. Swoop down low, and then fly around in a circle. Time to slow down! Bend down and land.
Big Box Basketball	Place an open box or laundry basket on a table or surface higher than chair level. Give your child a ball to throw overhand into the box or basket. You can also tie a ribbon across the tops of two chair backs with the box on the other side. Show your child how to throw the ball over the ribbon and into the box: "You did it! Hooray for you!"

Notes:

(hand) **Don't Forget!** Activities should be supervised at all times by an adult. Any material, food, or toy given to a young child should be reviewed for safety.

Fine Motor

Activities to Help Your Child Grow and Learn

Your child is becoming more skilled at buttoning and zipping clothing. He can use a fork and spoon to feed himself. He can spread soft butter, hummus, or jam on bread. He can hold a pencil or crayon with his thumb and two fingers and likes to draw. He may be able to draw circles or other simple shapes or letters.

Button-Up Bear	Let your child dress a large stuffed teddy bear or large doll. Make sure the clothes have a couple of large buttons or snaps to let your child practice small finger work. You might even find some baby shoes with Velcro or other similar closures. Tying or buckling shoes is probably too difficult right now. Say, "What a good Papa Bear you are!"
Beautiful Necklace	Cut small circles or flowers out of colored paper, and punch a hole in the center. Then, cut a large plastic soda straw into pieces. Let your child string the flowers and straw pieces with a shoelace. Show her how to make a pattern—flower, straw, flower, straw. She may not always repeat the pattern, but that is okay. Tie the ends, and she will have her own beautiful necklace!
Picking Peas	Buy a few fresh peapods at the market. Show your child how to find the peas inside the shell. Give him a few in a plastic container to shell for himself. When he is finished, rinse off the peas and eat them. Yum!
Sidewalk Artist	Let your child draw pictures on the sidewalk or driveway with colored outdoor chalk. You can also give your child a small paintbrush and let her paint a picture with water. The painting will be fun, and so will the magic of evaporation: "Where did your picture go?"
List Maker	Give your child a small pad of paper with a pencil or pen. Ask your child to help you make a shopping list. Let him write his own "words," and even draw pictures. When you get to the market, ask him to "read" his list. He is learning the magic of writing by putting meaning with his scribbles.
Little Snipper	Let your child practice cutting with safety scissors. Show her how to open and close the scissors while you hold the paper. Later, show her how to hold the scissors in one hand while she holds the paper with the other. At first, snipping edges is great progress. If she snips off a few pieces, save them in an envelope. Later, she can glue the little pieces on paper for a special art project!

Notes:

Don't Forget! Activities should be supervised at all times by an adult. Any material, food, or toy given to a young child should be reviewed for safety. Always watch your child during mealtime.

Problem Solving

Activities to Help Your Child Grown and Learn

Your busy learner is gaining many skills. She can put puzzles together (six pieces or maybe more), draw some shapes (circles and squares), and identify a few colors. She can match an object to a picture of that object and notices many similarities and differences. She is very curious about how things work, and your answers really help her understand and learn.

Box o' Blocks	Collect blocks and small boxes for your child to use for building. Build things together. Cardboard pieces make great roofs, and rulers or paint-stirring sticks make great bridges. Make a town. Add some toy cars and toy people. The town will come to life!
Picnic Memory Magic	Pretend that you are going on a picnic to help your child develop her memory. Say, "We're going on a picnic, and we're bringing apples." Encourage your child to think of the next item. "We're going on a picnic and we're bringing apples and (cookies)." Take turns and keep adding new items. How many items can she remember? This is great fun while riding in the car or on the bus!
Mr. Sticks	Ask your child to draw a stick figure on a paper plate or piece of cardboard. Say, "This is Mr. Sticks." Hide Mr. Sticks, and give your child clues to lead to Mr. Sticks: "He's in a room with water but not the bathroom. He's in a drawer near a door." Finding Mr. Sticks earns a big hug. Now it's your child's turn to give you clues.
Money Management	Make play money from green paper. Pretend to be the storekeeper and say, "Those socks cost $2. This lunch costs $3." Help your child count the right amount of money. Now let your child be the storekeeper. Add to the fun by collecting cereal boxes or empty milk cartons to make a store.
Picture Shopping List	Cut magazine or newspaper pictures of some foods you'll be shopping for. Place them in an empty envelope and take them to the supermarket. Let your child pull out the pictures and remind you of what you need. If he is holding a picture of eggs, say, "Yes, we need eggs today." When you buy the items, be sure to thank him for helping you remember!
Set the Table	Let your child help you set the table. Put a plate at each place. Now ask your child to count the plates. Ask your child to tell you how many spoons she will need. Help her count them out loud. As she gets better at counting, add other items: "How many napkins do we need? You are a very good helper."
Big, Bigger, Biggest!	Gather four or five shoes of different sizes. Make a line on the floor with tape or string, or draw a line on a large piece of paper. Ask your child to line up the shoes. Show him how to start with the smallest, then find the next biggest, then the next, until the biggest shoe is at the other end. Once he has the idea, gather up all the shoes again and mix them up. Ask him how fast he can line them up from smallest to biggest. Ready, set, go! Try this game with other items such as rocks or pinecones.

Notes:

Don't Forget! Activities should be supervised at all times by an adult. Any material, food, or toy given to a young child should be reviewed for safety.

Personal-Social

Activities to Help Your Child Grow and Learn

Your child is becoming more and more sociable. He can be very helpful with household tasks and can take care of many of his personal needs. He plays with other children but still needs support at times to cooperate and share. Your approval and attention are very important to him. He likes being silly and making others laugh, especially you.

Dress-Up Fun	Let your child play dress up in some old or interesting clothes. Boots are fun, as well as large hats, belts, and other accessories. A scarf or necklace adds a nice touch. A purse, wallet, or vest also makes the play interesting. Make sure there are some buttons to button, zippers to zip, or gloves to stick fingers into. Put a mirror at your child's level: "Where are you going today?"
Counting Turns	Help your child learn to manage taking turns by counting how long a turn will last. For example, tell your child he can swing until the count of 10 and then it will be his brother's turn. Count 10 swings out loud: "Okay, now it's your brother's turn for 10 swings. Help me count." Your child will learn that the wait for a turn will soon be over.
Wonderful Rhythm and Rock	Read or recite poems and rhymes to your child at special cozy quiet times. Cuddle up and rock a little to the rhythm of the words, or just cuddle and rock. Let your child fill in missing words to a familiar rhyme: "Humpty Dumpty sat on a…" Wall!
Cupcakes for All	Let your child help you bake cupcakes. She can sift, pour, and stir as much as she is able. Let her spread icing with a plastic knife. Talk about who the cupcake is for. Place it on a napkin and write that person's name on the napkin. Let your child share the special cupcakes.
Counting Goodnight Kisses	When you put your child to bed, count kisses out loud. Ask your child how many kisses for the chin: "Three? Okay, one [kiss], two [kiss], three [kiss]. How about your nose?" What a happy way to learn to count!
Counting Cars	Riding in the car or on the bus, ask your child to count all the blue cars he sees. Help him watch for blue cars and count them out loud. Remember, blue trucks don't count. Next time, let your child choose what to count!

Notes:

Don't Forget! Activities should be supervised at all times by an adult. Any material, food, or toy given to a young child should be reviewed for safety. Always watch your child during mealtime.

Communication

Activities to Help Your Child Grow and Learn

Your child now enjoys longer books and stories. She can help tell a story or make up silly stories of her own. She probably asks "why" often, not only about books but also about daily events. She can describe recent events with some detail. With a little help, she can place the events in order. She may be reading familiar signs in the neighborhood and may know what words and letters are. She knows her first and last name and probably recognizes her name in print.

Talking Book	Let your child cut out interesting pictures from a magazine or newspaper. Glue the pictures, one per page, in a notebook or on blank pages stapled together. Look through this picture book and ask your child to talk about the pictures: "Can you tell me about this picture? What colors do you see? Is that doggie happy or sad?" See if your child can tell you two or three things about each picture.
Say What You Can See	Riding the bus or in the car, look for things in a certain category. Find things with wheels, things that are tall, or things of different colors. Choose the category ahead of time or let your child pick. You might say, "Let's see how many animals we see." You and your child can point out live animals or animals on signs or billboards.
My Own Stories	Encourage your child to begin to make up stories of her own. Write them on a piece of paper as she tells them to you. She might like to draw or paint a picture to go along with the story. You can put these stories in a folder to make a book titled, "My Own Stories."
Fill in the Blank	When reading familiar stories or singing familiar songs, leave a word out and pause to let your child fill in the word or even the sound: "Twinkle, twinkle…[little star]."
Do What I Do	Do a simple action, such as clapping your hands. Tell your child, "Do what I do." Add a second motion such as patting your stomach. Have your child do it with you first, then by himself. Now add a third motion. See if your child can remember all three: clap, clap, pat, pat, wink, wink. Add more as long as your child can remember them and you both are having fun!
Rhyming Game	Try this little rhyming game. Say a word, such as *bake*. Ask your child to say a word that rhymes, such as *cake*. Now it's your turn: say *rake*. Help your child if she can't think of a word: "How about *take?*" When you run out of rhyming words, try another: "How about *cat?*" Sometimes you can put two words together: "Fat cat!" Have fun!

Notes:

Gross Motor
Activities to Help Your Child Grow and Learn

Your child is now more coordinated and will run, climb, swing, and balance with more confidence. He can jump, dance, and balance on one foot for longer than 1 second. He can walk heel to toe and begin to do forward somersaults. He may have the skills to pump on a swing.

Mystery Journey	In the house, outside, or at the park, ask your child to follow you on a mystery journey. You might go over to the cooler, around the blanket, hop across the grass, walk backward, and slide down a slide. When you finish, let her take a turn leading you through a mystery journey.
Catch	This is a good age to begin playing catch. Use a soft, medium-size ball (about 8 inches) that won't hurt if your child does not catch it. Remind him to put his arms out in front of him. Toss the ball to him from a close distance, then move back so that he can practice catching from 5 or 6 feet away. Good catch!
Music Melt	Play music and move around with your child (or several children). When you turn off the music, everyone should stop moving. Encourage your child to freeze in many different positions (on one foot, bent over, on tip toe). Say, "Melt," so that everyone can move again.
Bag Toss	Make a beanbag out of a knotted sock or bag filled with dry rice, small peas, or small pebbles. Ask your child to stand behind a line and toss the "bag" into a small box. As her aim gets better, move the target back a little. She can try to toss it underhand or throw it overhand.
Jumping	When your child can jump and land with two feet at the same time, show him how to jump over something with a little height of about 3 inches. Start with a book or blocks. See if your child can still keep two feet together: "You jumped high!"
Toddler T-Ball	Use an empty round ice cream carton, bucket, or any other safe round container as the stand for a medium-size ball or balloon. Let your child swing a small plastic bat or a cardboard roll from paper towels or gift wrap. When she hits the ball, she can run home—right into your arms!

Notes:

Don't Forget! Activities should be supervised at all times by an adult. Any material, food, or toy given to a young child should be reviewed for safety.

Fine Motor

Activities to Help Your Child Grow and Learn

42–48 months

Your child has stronger finger muscles and is more skilled in drawing and writing. She can put puzzle pieces or small toys together, such as interlocking blocks, and can string beads. She's getting better at using scissors and may be able to cut on a line without help. She may even be able to trace over simple designs.

Magazine Cutting and Pasting	Give your child pages from an old magazine, catalog, or junk mail, and a pair of small safety scissors. Let him cut pictures and glue them to a piece of paper. A glue stick works better when your child is learning. You can ask him to find certain kinds of pictures like favorite foods, fruit, cars, clothing, or animals.
Where's the Button?	Provide a couple of clothing items with large buttons for your child. You can also let her help you fasten a button on your clothes. Pretend it is a hide-and-seek game. The button hides first, then peeks out, and then comes through the hole: "There you are, Mr. Button Man! I got you!"
Wrap a Present	Give your child a small box, wrapping paper (or a colorful page from the newspaper), and clear tape. Cut the paper to a size your child can manage. Ask him to wrap the "present" and make believe you're going to give it to a friend. Your child can pull the paper up and around, then tape it to the box. You may have to help a little with the taping: "Look at that. You wrapped it yourself!"
Twisting and Turning	Save empty jars and the caps of catsup, mustard, jelly, or salt. Wash and dry everything well. Let your child match the correct cap to the bottle and twist it into place. Collect other types and sizes to add to the collection!
Tool Fun	Let your child play with tools. Show her how to screw a large nut onto a bolt. Let her try to hammer a short nail into a piece of soft wood after you start it. Help fit a fat screwdriver head into a large screw, turn it, and watch it go into something soft like soft wood or a cardboard box. Tell your child what a great builder she is!
Tub Scrub	After your child's bath, ask him to help you clean the tub by scrubbing all the way around the tub. Give your child a separate sponge or cloth just for this job. (No other cleansers, please). As the water drains out, your child can "scrub" the part of the tub where the water was. When finished, squeeze the cloth or sponge really hard! "Good helper!"
Artist at Work	Make a creative space for your child. Set up an area with clear boundaries where your child can explore materials such as paper, crayons, markers, glue, scissors, yarn pieces, stickers, and tape. Encourage her to create her art piece any way she wants to. Ask her to write her name on it or to show you where to write her name. Find a place to display it for all to see. Now, it's time to clean up!
Dough Fun	Make up a batch of playdough: 2 cups flour, 1 cup salt, 1 teaspoon oil, 1 cup water. Squish it all up with clean hands. Give your child a flat cookie sheet or placemat with a bit of flour on it to keep dough from sticking. Your child will enjoy pinching, pounding, rolling, and squeezing the dough. Add Popsicle sticks or a cookie cutter for more fun! Store in a plastic container in the refrigerator, and let your child help clean up with a damp cloth.

Notes:

Don't Forget! Activities should be supervised at all times by an adult. Any material, food, or toy given to a young child should be reviewed for safety. Always supervise your child using tools.

Problem Solving
Activities to Help Your Child Grow and Learn

Your child is learning to count things and can count up to three or four items. He can probably count up to 10 from memory. His knowledge about the world is growing. He now understands simple opposites such as up and down, and whether things are the same or different. He understands patterns or degrees of change, such as "cool, warm, hot" or "loud, louder, loudest."

Remember What Happened When
Encourage your child to tell you about things that happened in the past. You can start with this phrase: "Remember what happened when…(you suggest the event)?" Follow up with questions. "What did you like the best? What happened next? And then what happened?"

Guess Who?
At any quiet time, play this little guessing game. Think of someone your child knows well. Give clues one at a time to see if your child can guess who you are describing: "She has curly hair." When your child guesses correctly, switch turns. You might even describe the goldfish!

Color Hunt
Have a scavenger hunt for colors. Say, "Can you find something blue to bring me?" When your child returns, give her another color. If she brings back the wrong color, say, "You brought me a green sock. Can you find a blue sock?" You can give her clues, such as a piece of blue paper to hold while she looks for something blue.

Where Does It Go?
Put a glove or sock on your head or somewhere it doesn't belong. Ask, "Where is my glove?" When your child points or says it's on your head, ask him where it really belongs: "On my hand? Really?" Have fun with this silly game. Try another object, such as a bar of soap in a cereal bowl.

What Do You Do When
Ask your child simple questions, such as "What do you do when you're really tired?" "What do you do when you get hungry?" or "What do you do when you're all wet?" See if your child can give you answers that make sense. Talk about it.

What Doesn't Belong?
Gather three things that are very similar or in the same category, such as three lemons. Add a fourth item that does not belong, such as a bar of soap. Ask your child which one doesn't belong. You can also gather three things from the bathroom (soap, shampoo, toilet paper) and add something else, such as a screwdriver: "What doesn't belong? Why?"

Make a Rhyme
Play a rhyme game. You can make up the first part: "I picked up my *book* and started to…" Encourage your child to fill in the blank with a word that rhymes, such as *look*. Ask your child to quiz you, too!

Notes:

Personal-Social
Activities to Help Your Child Grow and Learn

Your child is better at taking turns and waiting. Although she plays with other children cooperatively, she still needs adult help from time to time to solve problems. Her feelings can be strong and may become easier to understand when you name them. She likes to select her own clothes and is more skilled at dressing herself.

Perfect Pouring

Give your child opportunities to pour at mealtimes. Give him a small pitcher or cup half filled with milk. Let him pour from the pitcher into his cup or bowl of cereal. Let him pour water, juice, or milk for himself and others at the table. Be patient, and have a paper towel ready just in case. Be sure to praise his success!

Dress-Up Party

Provide a variety of clothes to play with—nothing fancy, just oversized shirts, scarves, hats, skirts, shoes, or even loose fabric. Choose a theme, such as going to the beach or getting ready for a party. Have your child search for objects or props. Pick out your own outfit once your child has selected hers. Children love to imitate adults in their family and community. Encourage her to dress herself by fastening buttons, snaps, zippers, and so forth. Play along: "Are you going to a party?"

Playful Puppets

Puppets are great for pretend fun. Use store-bought puppets or make your own. Find or draw a picture of a person or animal, cut it out, and paste it on cardboard. Attach a Popsicle stick, paint-stirring stick, or chopstick for a handle. Draw a face on the bottom of a paper lunch bag and put your hand up into the folds. Move your fingers and make it "talk." Let your child be one character and you can be another. Have conversations in pretend voices.

Special Helper

Tell your child he is your special helper. Let him help you wash the clothes, cook, feed pets, sweep, and wash dishes. He can help in some small way with almost everything. Be sure to allow extra time since young helpers may need it. This helping may become part of your child's family chores. Be sure to give a lot of praise and keep it fun.

Choice Time

Offer choices to your child about her activities, including taking care of herself. You might offer her the choice to brush her teeth either before or after she puts on pajamas. You can also let her pick a snack from two options. It's more fun and easier if she has some choice in how things happen.

Soothing a Playmate

When young children play together, often one child will get a bump or feel injured in some way. Show your child how to comfort a friend in distress with a gentle touch or a little hug. Teach your child some comfort words, such as, "Are you okay?" This empathy will be a valuable lesson in making and keeping friends.

Feeling Faces

Act out different feelings with your child. Be happy, sleepy, sad, silly, surprised, and frustrated! Show your child a deep frown, a giggle, or pretend to cry and have him guess what you are feeling. Now have your child try with you!

Notes:

Don't Forget! Activities should be supervised at all times by an adult. Any material, food, or toy given to a young child should be reviewed for safety. Always watch your child during mealtime.

Communication

Activities to Help Your Child Grow and Learn

Your child is learning new words every day, and he enjoys playing with language by rhyming words. He may use very silly language and laugh at his own jokes. He uses a lot of inflection (changes in his voice) when he describes events. He knows the difference between day and night, today and tomorrow. He can carry out three or more simple directions. He knows that printed letters and words mean something to others.

Putting on a Play	Create a story or a play with a few puppets. Have a conversation with them, taking turns asking and answering questions. Put on a puppet show of a familiar story or folktale. Talk about the characters, assign roles, and enjoy a wonderful play!
Adventure Pals	Take a special trip someplace new. Visit a museum, a park or outdoor area, a store, or a library. Plan with your child. Talk about what you will be seeing and doing. After you come home, ask questions about what she saw and what she did. Encourage her to tell other family members about the outing. If you have a camera, take photos to show others what you saw on your adventure.
Dramatic Storytime	Read a favorite story to your child. Ask him what happened at the beginning, middle, and end. Have your child act out the story and be different characters. If you read a story about farm animals, he could pretend to be a cow, chicken, pig, or horse. Encourage him to act out the beginning, the middle, and the end of the story.
All About Me	Have your child make a book about herself. Staple or put together several pieces of paper with tape, yarn, or ribbon. She can glue pictures of family members on a *family* page and things she likes on a *favorite things* page. She can trace her hand or draw pictures. Have your child plan her book, make it, then "read" you her story or tell you about each picture.
Cleanup Helper	Your child will enjoy helping you around the house. At mealtime, he could help set the table. Ask him to help sweep an area or put toys away. Be sure to allow plenty of time. In the morning, your child can put his own nightclothes into their special place. Look around for little tasks in your own home. Your child will be proud of helping the family!
I Can, I Can, I Can!	Challenge your child to remember and do three things in a single direction. Ask your child to go into the bathroom, flush the toilet, and bring your toothbrush! You can also ask her to find your fuzzy blanket, wrap it around a book, and put it on the sofa. Or ask her to find a shoe, put a block in it, and put it under the table: "Can you do it? Yeah!"
Cloudy Friends	This activity is fun on a day when the sky is filled with puffy clouds. Go outside and lie on your back and take turns pointing out different cloud shapes and patterns. Ask your child what the clouds look like: "Look. There's an ice cream cone! What do you see?"

Notes:

 Don't Forget! Activities should be supervised at all times by an adult. Any material, food, or toy given to a young child should be reviewed for safety.

Gross Motor

Activities to Help Your Child Grow and Learn

48–54 months

Your child is continuing to develop and refine her gross motor skills. She can ride a tricycle or bike with training wheels, weaving in and out of obstacles, and stopping and turning with skill. She can kick a ball you roll into her path. She is learning to run and change direction without stopping and to somersault and gallop. She can keep herself going on a swing by pumping her legs back and forth and can throw a ball overhead about 10 feet.

Air Balloon	Play this game with your child and a couple of his friends. Keep a balloon in the air by tapping it up. As it comes down, it's someone else's turn to tap it. See how long you can keep the balloon from falling to the ground.
Target Practice	Cut a few 8- to 9-inch holes in a big piece of cardboard to make a target. You also can draw a target with chalk on a sidewalk or pick a target, such as a tree. Let your child try to throw a bean-bag or ball through the holes or at the target. Have your child start very close to the target and then move back a few feet. Let him try throwing underhand and then overhand. Be sure to cheer when he hits the target!
Ball Games	Your child is ready to practice ball skills. A basket on a chair can be a hoop for a basketball. Use a big ball and show your child how to dribble and shoot to make a basket. Play soccer using any two objects for goals and kicking the ball to get a goal.
Scarf Dancing	On a rainy day, turn on some music. Your child can dance while holding and waving scarves or dishtowels. Try different kinds of music. Encourage her to listen and move to the rhythm and mood of the music.
Circle Catch	It's fun to play catch with your child and a few friends. Use a beach ball or something a little smaller. Show the children how to hold out their arms to get ready for the ball. Stand in a circle and throw the ball to each other. Get ready. Now catch!
Playground Time	Bring your child to a neighborhood playground, park, or open grassy area as often as possible. He will enjoy climbing, running, swinging, sliding, and learning new skills. Keep a close watch. He might be very daring!

Notes:

Don't Forget! Activities should be supervised at all times by an adult. Any material, food, or toy given to a young child should be reviewed for safety.

Fine Motor

Activities to Help Your Child Grow and Learn

48–54 months

Your child's finger movements are more controlled now. He can put small toys together and build a tower of 8 or more small blocks. He is learning how to draw shapes if you show him how first and may be learning how to write some letters. He can cut out circles and shapes with curved lines using safety scissors. As he gets more control over his hands, he is able to do more by himself.

Pudding Fun	Make a batch of pudding. Place a few spoonfuls on a cookie sheet or plate. (You may want to cover the table with newspaper first.) Have your child wash her hands and then finger-paint in the pudding. Draw pictures and practice drawing shapes or letters in the pudding. The best part is cleaning up! Yum!
Little Author	Ask your child to make his own book. Identify a theme and find materials. Attach together a few pieces of paper. Your child can draw pictures or paste magazine photos to illustrate a story. Encourage him to tell you his story: events he remembers, his likes and dislikes, and who his friends are. Help him write his words on each page.
Signed by the Artist	Have your child paint or draw a picture. When your child finishes, help her write her name. She may need help at first, but then she can try to do it by herself. Encourage her to make marks on the paper, even if they don't look "just right." Your child will learn by doing activities on her own!
Paper Chains	Cut paper into strips about 1 inch by 5 inches to make paper chains. Show your child how to make a loop by gluing or taping the ends together. Start a chain by inserting the next strip through the first loop. See how long you can make the chain. Use this chain to count down to an important event by removing the links, one day at a time!
You Have Mail	Let your child open the junk mail. He can exercise his fingers opening the mail, and he may find some little surprises inside. Help your child write and mail letters to family members or to a favorite performer or athlete.
Water Pictures	On a dry, warm day, give your child a plastic bucket of water, a paintbrush, and an old sponge. On a safe paved driveway, fence, or sidewalk, let her paint pictures with the water on the cement or wood. Watch the pictures disappear as the water evaporates: "What happened?"

Notes:

Don't Forget! Activities should be supervised at all times by an adult. Any material, food, or toy given to a young child should be reviewed for safety.

ASQ-3™ Learning Activities by Elizabeth Twombly and Ginger Fink.
Copyright © 2013 by Paul H. Brookes Publishing Co. All rights reserved.

115

Problem Solving

Activities to Help Your Child Grow and Learn

Your child's attention span is growing. She can attend to an activity she enjoys without supervision. She is starting to sort according to shape, size, and length and can match items that look alike. She is learning how things go together on the basis of function. For example, she can point to "things for drawing" in a picture of multiple objects. Your child loves to read stories and is learning how to make up stories or story endings by herself. Wild stories and exaggerations are common.

Riddle, Riddle	Tell your child to use his brain and solve these riddles. "Can you name an animal that gives us something to drink?" (cow) "Can you think of something that flies but doesn't have wings?" (flag, rocket, kite) "Can you think of something that rolls but doesn't have wheels?" (ball, orange) If your child can't think of an answer, give hints until he gets it. Now, ask your child to make up a riddle for you.
Grouping and Sorting	Gather together a lot of little things in a small container: paper clips, rubber bands, barrettes, or odds and ends. Talk with your child about ways to group the things together. Sort rubber bands by color, size, or length. Line up five items, and point to each one as you count. Now let your child try.
Waiting Game	As you wait for something, count together to see how long it will take to happen. When you are on the bus waiting for the light to change to green, count how long it takes to change. Your child will learn how to count, and it may help her become more patient.
Feely Bag	Gather small familiar objects from outside or around your house and put them in a paper bag. Try a small leaf, a baseball, or your child's toothbrush. Let your child reach into the bag and pick an item without looking. When your child's hand is in the bag touching the item, ask him to guess what it is. Help him if he has a difficult time naming the item.
Number and Letter Search	Play number and letter searches at the store. Encourage your child to find numbers or letters on walls, pictures, and signs. When she spots one, say, "You found the number 5. Good for you!" Point out numbers or single letters of the alphabet. She can start to learn the sounds of letters. "You found an A. It makes an 'ah' sound. Aaapple…apple!"
What Comes Next?	Make a simple repeating pattern with your child with small toys, blocks, utensils, pasta, or shoes. Line up items to start the pattern. Have him help you finish it. Encourage your child to complete the pattern and help if he gets stuck: "This pattern starts with a shoe, then a block, then a noodle. What do you think comes next?"

Notes:

ASQ-3™ Learning Activities by Elizabeth Twombly and Ginger Fink.
Copyright © 2013 by Paul H. Brookes Publishing Co. All rights reserved.

Personal-Social

Activities to Help Your Child Grow and Learn

48–54 months

Your child is becoming more independent in dressing. He can put his shoes on the correct feet. He uses the toilet without help and can brush his teeth with a "touch up" from you. He is eating different types of foods and can serve himself at the table, pouring and scooping without spilling. He can play cooperatively with other children and will comfort a playmate in distress. He plays games with rules and can follow directions.

Game Time	Your child may enjoy learning games that have rules. You can play card games and board games with your child. If other children join you, play with them at first to help them learn about rules and taking turns. Start a family game night: one night a week after dinner!
Super Chef	Your child will love to help you cook or make her own snack. She can learn how to pour, stir, spread, and cut soft foods with your help. You might try mini-pizzas. Your child can scoop spaghetti sauce on an English muffin or bagel, sprinkle on some cheese, and add toppings that she likes. Cook the pizzas in the oven for a few minutes (you do this part). Yum!
Tent Safari	On a rainy day, ask your child if he would like to invite a friend over to play. Have the children build a tent by draping old sheets or blankets over furniture. Once they make their tent, they can play in it or read books with a flashlight. What fun to have a secret hideaway! Children this age can help pick up. They can help you fold the sheets by finding a corner and bringing it to you!
Teddy Bear Picnic	Have your child bring stuffed animals or dolls on a picnic. Make a basket with a blanket, napkins, pretend food, and plastic plates and tea cups. Your child (and the bears!) can get "dressed up" for the picnic. Your child can help clean up after a wonderful picnic.
Everybody Loves a Letter!	Have your child write a letter to someone he knows. You can write the words he wants to say, or your child can try writing. He can also draw a picture. Help him write his name at the end of the letter. Show him how to address an envelope (you may need to do this part). Let him add the stamp and really mail the letter. Watch the mail for a happy reply.
Rub-a-Dub	Keep a footstool in the bathroom so that your child can step up and see herself in the mirror. Give your child her own washcloth and towel, and teach her how to wash her face. Give her a big kiss on her clean and shiny face! At bath time, she can wash and dry herself, too. Don't forget to have her brush her teeth with your help.

Notes:

👆 **Don't Forget!** Activities should be supervised at all times by an adult. Any material, food, or toy given to a young child should be reviewed for safety. Always watch your child during mealtime and bath time.

Communication

Activities to Help Your Child Grow and Learn

Your child's communication skills are growing. She is learning how to have conversations with people she knows. She can start conversations as well as respond to people's questions. She is learning different parts of speech and using more complex sentences. When describing something, she might say, "It was a very big brown dog." She may use silly language and laugh at her own jokes.

Animal Crossing	This game is for the whole family. Cut pictures of animals from a magazine. Turn the pictures face down. Have one person choose a picture. The other people ask yes-or-no questions to guess what the animal is: "Does the animal swim? Is it bigger than a cat?" After someone guesses correctly, another person chooses a picture and lets the others guess.
Bedtime Memories	At bedtime each night, have a soft talk with your child. Whisper to him, "What was your favorite thing that happened today?" Ask what else happened. Share your favorite event, too.
Reading Adventures	Read to your child every day. Read slowly and with interest, with expression and voices. Use a finger to follow the words. Stop reading at times. Encourage your child to talk about the pictures and the story. "Who is your favorite character? What happened in the middle of the story?" Make this a special together time!
Moonbeams	When the moon is visible, find a place to look at the moon and stars with your child. Explore your child's imagination: "What do you see? Can you connect the stars to make a picture? What do you think it is like on the moon? What would you do there? How would you feel about being so far away from Earth?"
Strike Up the Band	Have your child chant or sing a nursery rhyme and tap it out on a drum, the bottom of a pot, or a small box. Make this activity more challenging and interesting by adding new instruments such as bells, spoons, or shakers. Have some noisy fun with friends!
At the Office	Set up an office for your child with notebooks, a toy phone, an old keyboard, pencils and pens, a ruler, a calculator, and a calendar. Add envelopes, paper, and stickers. Encourage her to pretend to go to work, write letters, type messages, and make notes. Pretend with her. Call on the phone and ask questions: "When will the mail come today?"

Notes:

Don't Forget! Activities should be supervised at all times by an adult. Any material, food, or toy given to a young child should be reviewed for safety.

121

Gross Motor
Activities to Help Your Child Grow and Learn

Your child continues to develop and refine his gross motor skills. He is much more stable and is learning how to balance on one foot or walk along a narrow beam. He is learning skills such as jumping, hopping on one foot, and skipping. He will enjoy activities such as throwing, catching, and kicking balls. He can ride a small bike with training wheels. Watch him closely because he may try some dangerous tricks.

The Stone and the River	Get a group of children together. The person who is "it" tries to tag other children. If a child is tagged, she must turn into a "stone" (not move). Another child may turn a stone player into a "river" by touching her. A river player can run around again. Whoever is frozen three times is the next "it." This is great for exercise!
Leaf Fun	Go outside with your child to play in the leaves in your yard or at a park. Try catching the leaves as they fall. Collect and sort leaves of different colors, sizes, and shapes. Rake leaves into small piles. Chase each other around the piles, jump in them, or try to leap over them.
Splash Game	On a hot day, have a sponge relay with large sponges and buckets of water. Divide children into two teams. Place two sets of two buckets at opposite ends of an open space. Fill one set with water. The children race to dip their sponge in the water, carry it to the empty bucket, and squeeze the water out. The first team to fill their bucket wins! You can also play catch with the wet sponges.
Ribbon Dance	Cut ribbon or streamers into 6-foot lengths. Show your child how to dance and make designs in the air. Try circles and loops, up and down movements, and figure eights. Try the movements with two ribbons, one in each hand. Move from place to place taking the ribbons with you. Put on music to make a "ribbon dance." Skip, run, and walk!
Animal Games	Turn pictures of animals face down, and take turns choosing an animal. Act out the animal you picked. Your child has to guess what animal you are. For a kangaroo, you must jump, jump, jump. For a cheetah, you will run. Act like a giraffe by walking on tiptoes and stretching really tall.
Crazy Catch Game	For this funny game of catch, gather a ball, a small pillow or cushion, a stuffed animal, a shoe, and a small box. From a distance of about 4 feet, toss each item to your child. See if she can catch each one. Move back 6 feet. What a good catcher!
Bottle Bowling	Collect six plastic bottles of similar size. Put a handful of dry peas or gravel in each one and cap it tightly. Arrange the bottles in a bowling game shape: three bottles in the back row, two bottles in the middle, and one bottle in the front. Show your child where to stand, about 4 feet back, and "bowl" with a soft medium-sized ball. Take as many turns as needed to knock them down: "Strike!"

Notes:

Don't Forget! Activities should be supervised at all times by an adult. Any material, food, or toy given to a young child should be reviewed for safety.

 ASQ-3

Fine Motor
Activities to Help Your Child Grow and Learn

54–60 months

Your child is able to use her fingers with more control. Her finger movements are coordinated and faster. She may be able to write some or all of the letters of her name. She may begin to prefer using one hand over the other. Your child can cut shapes with scissors and is getting better at buttoning and tying her shoes.

Lacing Cards	Your child can use safety scissors to cut simple pictures from magazines and glue them onto cardboard. Punch several holes around the outside of the cardboard. Tie a shoestring or yarn through one of the holes. Make a firm tip with tape at the other end. Show your child how to sew, in and out, around the edge. He can try to sew two cards together.
Picture Perfect	Help your child make a picture frame for a favorite photo. Cut out two rectangles of stiff paper, a little larger than the picture. On one, cut a rectangle inside that's smaller than the picture border. Let your child decorate the smaller "frame" with stickers, glitter, shells, macaroni, or anything small and interesting. Glue the photo to the large solid rectangle. Place the decorated "frame" over the picture and glue the edges. Beautiful!
Bird Café	Find a medium pinecone or corncob. Let it dry. Have your child use a plastic knife to spread peanut butter on it. Roll it in bird seed, sunflower seeds, or crushed granola. Hang it on a string under a tree or outside a window. Watch the birds discover your wonderful gift to them. Count how many different types of birds come to the Bird Café!
Map It	Make a map of your neighborhood. Go for a walk and point out streets, buildings, parks, or other landmarks. Use paper and markers to make a map. You may need to help your child start her map. Begin by mapping your house or her room. Ask your child, "Where would we put your bed on the map? How about your toy box?"
Cutting Shapes	Draw a pattern or shape, such as a circle or a triangle, with a pencil on a piece of paper. Have your child use child-safe scissors to cut out the pattern. When he can follow the pattern, draw larger or more complex ones. Make fun shapes, such as a teddy bear or a train!
Make a Sculpture	Create a sculpture with your child. Use materials you find in your home and outside—plastic bottles, newspaper, twigs, jar lids, paper plates, Popsicle sticks, boxes, plastic containers, bits of ribbon, and fabric. Give your child masking tape, small wire, duct tape, and some glue for joining materials together. Put materials in a place where your child can "create" for a few days and where this wonderful sculpture can dry.
Fancy Bananas	When seated at a table, give your child a smooth ripe banana and a ballpoint pen. Show your child how to draw a face at one end. Draw some clothes with buttons and a belt. Have fun decorating the banana. Now peel it and eat!

Notes:

 Don't Forget! Activities should be supervised at all times by an adult. Any material, food, or toy given to a young child should be reviewed for safety.

Problem Solving

Activities to Help Your Child Grow and Learn

Your child can count to at least 15 from memory and can accurately count at least 10 objects. He is able to follow directions in a group activity and knows the rules at home and at school. He enjoys pretend play and may act out different roles with friends. Wild stories and exaggerations are common. He enjoys reading books and may have simple books memorized. He is starting to understand how things work in the world and is curious about why things are the way they are.

Pretzel Fun	Have fun making pretzel letters (or numbers). Wash your hands, then cut pizza dough into strips. Help your child form numbers or letters with the dough. Show her how to brush with a beaten egg, sprinkle with salt, and bake until golden brown. Tell your child the sounds that the letters make. Eat up an *A, B,* or *C!*
Fun Food Coloring	Let your child experiment with food coloring in his food. It only takes a small drop! Color scrambled eggs blue. Color a glass of milk red. Add a drop of green to a piece of apple or to a slice of bread before toasting it. Color mashed potatoes yellow. Ask your child for ideas!
How Long? How Many?	Count how long or how many times your child can do a new skill, such as standing on one foot or bouncing a ball. Celebrate doing a new skill for a little more time. Let her count while you try balancing a book on your head. Help your child practice new skills and counting.
Storytime Acting	Tell your child a story using different voices, body postures, facial expressions, or even hats to be different characters. Now it's your child's turn to tell a story. Encourage your little one to ham it up—and don't forget to be a good audience.
What's Missing?	Give your child time to look at a group of five or more different toys. Hide a single toy and ask, "Which toy is missing?" You may need to give clues at first. Once he guesses correctly, hide a different toy. Let him hide a toy for you. It's his turn to try to trick you!
Find the Treasure	Plan this activity ahead of time. Hide "treasure" (a favorite snack, a bag of crayons, some stickers) in a place your child can reach. Draw the place you want your child to search for each "treasure." Be sure to make the drawings simple and clear. Your child will have great fun with the treasure map. Celebrate when your child finds the treasure!

Notes:

Don't Forget! Activities should be supervised at all times by an adult. Any material, food, or toy given to a young child should be reviewed for safety. Always watch your child during mealtime.

Personal-Social
Activities to Help Your Child Grow and Learn

54–60 months

Your child is able to meet most of her personal needs. She may need practice or help on more difficult tasks, such as tying her shoes. She eats a variety of foods, has social dining skills, and dresses herself. She enjoys playing with other children and working together on projects. She is beginning to use her words to help solve conflicts with friends.

Going on a Date	Go on a "date" to lunch or a movie with your child. Before you go out, you can get ready. He can put on a special shirt, wash his hands and face, use the potty, and brush his teeth. Show him a mirror so he can see how great he looks. Now go have fun! Be extra polite. Say "please" and "thank you" throughout your date.
Fruit Salad	Make a fruit salad for lunch with any favorite fruits such as grapes, bananas, apples, and oranges. Your child will enjoy washing or peeling the fruit. She could help slice a banana with a plastic knife. Add yummy things to the salad, such as yogurt or sunflower seeds. Your child can practice using a spoon and fork to make and serve the fruit salad.
Pressed Flower Cards	Collect flowers from your yard, neighborhood, a park, or a roadside. Flowers that are small and delicate work best. Place the flowers between sheets of paper towels or newspaper, then lay them between heavy books. Give the flowers a few days to dry and flatten out. Glue them to a piece of paper to make notecards. Help your child write someone a special note.
911	Talk to your child about what to do if he gets lost or if there is an emergency. Teach your child his name, address, and telephone number. Your child can learn how to dial 911. Role-play using a pretend phone, but teach your child to use a real phone for a real emergency. It may help if he learns this information as a song. Make a card for your child that has his name, address, phone number, emergency contact, and a list of any allergies in case you cannot be reached. Give your child his own wallet to carry the card in his pocket or backpack.
I Can Dress Myself	Make sure your child has a little extra time in the morning to get dressed. Encourage her to try to button her shirt, snap her pants, or tie her shoes. She will need help and some time, but be patient. The more she practices, the sooner she will be able to get dressed all by herself.
You as Me, Me as You	You and your child can switch roles. He can pretend to help you get dressed or brush your hair. This pretend time could include a change of small jobs, clothes, behaviors, vocabulary, and other habits. Keep the activity positive and fun.

Notes:

Don't Forget! Activities should be supervised at all times by an adult. Any material, food, or toy given to a young child should be reviewed for safety. Always watch your child during mealtime.

129